Winning
in a Highly Competitive Manufacturing Environment

Ronald L. Buckley

Shady Brook Press
Norwalk, CT

*Winning in a Highly Competitive
Manufacturing Environment*
Copyright © 2003 Ronald L. Buckley

Book, Jacket Design and Printing by

Falcon Books
San Ramon, California

ISBN 0-9727881-0-7

Except for brief quotes used in reviews, no part of this book
may be reproduced by any means without the written
permission of the publisher.

Shady Brook Press
5 Shady Brook Lane
Norwalk CT 06854

PRINTED IN THE UNITED STATES OF AMERICA

DEDICATION and ACKNOWLEDGMENT

I dedicate this effort to the marvelous men and women that I have had the great privilege of working with over the last thirty plus years. I also acknowledge their contribution to this work. I profoundly hope that this book conveys the tremendous respect and gratitude I have for these people and their efforts.

A special thanks to my wife, for her support in this effort.

CONTENTS

Part 1 Background
Chapter 1   History · 11

Part 2 The Factory
Chapter 2   The Way I See It · · · · · · · · · · · · · · · · · · 21
Chapter 3   Linked-cell Manufacturing · · · · · · · · · · · · · · 35
Chapter 4   Inventory Flexibility and Reduction · · · · · · · · 47
Chapter 5   Velocity · 63
Chapter 6   The In-house Store · · · · · · · · · · · · · · · · · 77
Chapter 7   The "Bread Man Routine" · · · · · · · · · · · · · 85
Chapter 8   Wand-to-order · 93
Chapter 9   Letters of Intent · · · · · · · · · · · · · · · · · · 103
Chapter 10   Point of Use · 111
Chapter 11   Certified Vendors · · · · · · · · · · · · · · · · · 121
Chapter 12   Monitoring Labor Costs and Controlling
             Other Costs · 129
Chapter 13   Creating Equipment Flexibility · · · · · · · · · · · 141
Chapter 14   Creating Labor Flexibility Through Training · · · 155
Chapter 15   Andon Lights · 165
Chapter 16   e-business · 169

Part 3 Quality
Chapter 17   Quality and First-Pass Yield · · · · · · · · · · · · 179
Chapter 18   Quality and Statistical Process Control · · · · · · 199
Chapter 19   Quality and Mistake Proofing (Poka-yoke) · · · · 211
Chapter 20   Quality and Out-of-Box Failure Elimination · · · 219

Part 4 Teams
Chapter 21   Cross-Functional Self-Directed Teams · · · · · · · 229

Epilogue   A Final Word · 253
Appendix A · 259
Appendix B · 271
Appendix C · 279
Appendix D · 281

PREFACE

In this book I will use simple language to describe a step-by-step process that can be used to create a very efficient money-making manufacturing organization that will be able to compete with the best of companies in the new Millennium. To make a sometimes-dull topic interesting, I will draw on my thirty plus years of past manufacturing experiences and share my real life challenges in describing situations that everyone involved in manufacturing can relate to.

I will explore the idea that working with and believing in a process of continuous improvement is rewarding not only as a means to improve profits, but also as a means to achieve great personal satisfaction by developing your employees' knowledge and skills while at the same time providing real job security within their own abilities. In this book I talk about the progress that can be made through the implementation of Lean-flow Manufacturing techniques with linked-cells and quality programs like Statistical Process Control and Six Sigma. I show how these productivity-improving ideas create flexibility and improve throughput velocity. I will detail how these programs can be implemented by simply involving your employees through "Cross-Functional Self-Directed Teams." The Team's accomplishments will leave them with the self-confidence that contributes so much toward creating a workforce that is secure and happy in their work. Happy employees look forward to coming to work. They not only show up regularly, but also are continually striving to improve the Company's competitive position. Employee development is no longer a luxury that is reserved for the IBMs and GEs of the manufacturing world; it is a necessity for all companies of any size that intend to remain competitive in the new Millennium.

I endeavor to demonstrate that if a company is going to be successful in the new Millennium and in the future, it must use and optimize all the productive resources at its disposal. These include all its employees' talents through employee involvement in a proactive manner at all levels. The "Cross-Functional Self-Directed Team" is one way to win at the competition game. Invest in, train and engage all your people in improving your business. Employees will get involved in a proactive way, if they believe they share in and are part of what is going on in your company. They hunger to be part of the scene and will respond when treated well and like adults who can deal with the realities that affect their jobs.

I hope the investment made in reading the following pages proves to be fruitful not only to the reader but also to all those individuals over whom the reader has direct and indirect influence.

PART 1
BACKGROUND

CHAPTER 1

History

It is my bold and profound hope to grab the interest of my readers by using the examples of the many lessons I learned while in the employ of some of this country's best companies: United States Surgical Corporation, now a division of Tyco; Raytheon Medical Systems, a division of the Raytheon Company; Novametrix Medical Systems, now a division of Respironics Inc.; Marquette Medical Systems, Inc. and General Electric Medical Systems Information Technology, part of General Electric. I trust that these lessons will stimulate and encourage others to embark on a mission of continuous improvement through the use of modern methods of business management and manufacturing improvement. Also, on these pages one can glean a recipe for having great fun while pursuing industrial greatness.

Although throughout this book I refer often to the lessons that were learned at these great companies, I have spent considerable time consulting and working inside these companies and their subsidiaries, as well as outside these companies. In addition I have spent countless hours talking with peers from other companies and various professional organizations. To these experiences I must add the fortunate opportunities I have had working with various consulting firms.

I have two main reasons for using my personal experiences as examples in this book. First, some of the divisions of these companies were the exemplar models of companies operating in what I call the '70s or '80s mode. In other words, they were teetering on the brink of extinction with poor profits, high scrap rates, obsolete processes and poor Management methods – the perfect example of employee un-involvement, until the awakening. Second, I use these examples to make a sometimes dull and impersonal subject take on an aspect of life and excitement as the reader identifies with the characters and situations used as examples.

Historical Background

More than one of these companies can trace their histories back to the beginning of the last century and one of these companies, like so many businesses of that day, was a family business paternalistic toward their employees, treating them as an extension of their own family. This attitude was evidenced by the exceptional benefits their workers enjoyed. An employees' benefit trust gave each employee with three or more years of service an equity position in the business. Also there were company picnics, holiday parties, free milk every day, attendance bonuses and invitations to the family estate. The money that was collected from Company vending machines was used to fund an Employees Association that ran Company bingo games, sent fruit baskets to the sick, sponsored dinner parties and just about any social event the imagination could conjure up.

After the company was acquired by a multinational company in the '50s, not much changed. Employees who held equity positions were given the new company's stock in trade. After the acquisition, there was more money available for investment. Yet, in fact, change in the way the business was run came slowly over the next two decades.

History

Like many businesses in America after World War II, this company was very successful, and foreign competition was virtually nonexistent. There were few reasons to question the Management techniques that had been so successful for so long. Profits just kept rolling in, pleasing "Mother" (the new owner) and lending credence to her policy of limited interference. It was enough just to keep up with technology by adding new equipment and developing new products with more new features. Not many people were very interested in revolutionary ideas like continuous improvement, flow manufacturing, Kanban, Statistical Process Control, Six Sigma, work simplification and total employee involvement. Well, I must confess, the first time it was suggested that we take control of the factory away from the foremen and turn the process over to the people, I thought the person who was making the suggestion was something less than an idiot. I became a believer, but only after many years of frustration with the old system.

In the Pages That Follow

Ahead I will describe what it is like to take a company from operating in the '70s or '80s mode, with its attendant problems, to a very efficient and exciting company prepared to meet and defeat the competition in the new Millennium. Topics covered will be world class continuous improvement methods such as: Lean-flow Manufacturing techniques, linked-cell manufacturing, factory Kanban, vendor Kanban, in-house store, "Bread Man routine," Wand-to-order, certified vendors, point-of-use storage, material backflushing and cross training to create flexibility. I will also cover improving competitiveness by: reducing purchase costs, low cost country sourcing, vendor pull contracts, supplier partnerships, leading in vendor negotiations and e-auctions. Also included are quality improvement techniques through Six Sigma, Statistical Process Control, Poka-yoke – mistake proofing, Out-of-Box Failure elimination, warranty expense reduction and first-pass yield improvement. Other areas of focus will include: inventory reduction, product velocity acceleration, on-time Customer delivery, floor space reduction, establishing "Cross-Functional Self-Directed" Work Teams, employee evaluation, energizing employees, and improving Union relations.

Prevailing attitudes of companies operating in the '70s/ '80s mode will be explored. The process of waking up to the realization that change is necessary to a company's survival is frustrating. Others in the organization will still be resistant to change. Management support is essential to the success of any major change in the way an organization functions. Consultants can help and sometimes are necessary, if only to convince others in the organization that Management is serious. Great care should be exercised when selecting a consulting firm. Over the years I have used several excellent firms.

One of the better consulting firms I have used was initially called to one of the multi-plant facilities I was part of in the 1980s for a general review and to assist with improving the factory layout. What the firm found was tremendous opportunity. Their proposals just made good sense. They were packed with down to earth realistic solutions with huge payback potential. They ended up doing an in-depth overall operations review and detail layout that consolidated all operations previously spread over five buildings into one building. This first phase was so successful that the firm was asked to assist in the implementation of a pull manufacturing system we called "Straight Through Processing." We used the term "Straight Through Processing" to avoid any link to the term "Just-in-Time," which at the time was thought to be a purely Japanese invention and as such met with considerable resistance. The same firm was also contracted for the implementation of Statistical Process Control, Six Sigma's predecessor in the factory. I can't express the delight I experienced with this last program. To see employees with less than a high school education putting together presentations for top Management on their own time after-hours in a Union shop and then carrying them off in such a sincere and professional manner is like experiencing a high that is beyond description. God, I loved those people for their efforts. These employee involvement programs were the most incredibly beautiful parts of my career. Once you get a taste of this kind of working environment you need more; it is addictive in the most positive way.

By the time the Consultants were wrapping up the first phase of the general operations review and the plant layout, we had made much progress but still had a fair way to go; however, by then we knew what was possible – anything we put our minds to.

Not all the players on the top Management Team believed that these ideas of employee involvement would work. I remember one incident that took place at an off-site Management meeting involving all Management down to the foreman level. The American Hockey Team's defeat of the Russian Hockey Team in the 1980 Olympics had been commonly referred to as a miracle. Wanting to capitalize on this event to draw inspiration from the win we used it to create an analogy between the American Hockey Team and our Management Team. The comment from a senior employee, after the analogy was made, was: "At least the American hockey players knew how to skate." I am sure there were others on our Team who were convinced that we didn't even have ice in our rink. Before it was over our players did learn how to skate and win while having a lot of fun doing it.

The decision was made to move ahead with most of the Consultants' recommendations. First came the systems improvements and execution of the new plant layout. Then came the real fun, the cultural change that comes with adopting a system that turns the manufacturing process over to the people. The Self-Directed Team approach and Statistical Process Control (SPC), more than anything else, were responsible for changing the culture in this facility.

The flow manufacturing Just-in-Time effort helped to bring all the various programs into proper focus by defining how they were all related and capitalizing on the Self-Directed Team approach already being used in the SPC program.

The cultural changes didn't come easily. Many foremen gave lip service to the new programs but did little to support them. Still others were openly critical to the point of being obstructionists. The great thing about employee involvement and Self-Directed Teams is that once the Team is turned on to the process even the obstructionists can't stop the forward momentum of the missionaries. Eventually the foremen relinquished control to their people. When the results started to roll in, everyone hopped on the proverbial bandwagon. Management started listening to the people and why not? Problems that previously had plagued the foremen for years were being resolved, scrap rates were dropping, and it was fun to come to work in the morning. These people were the best chance the company had to succeed at beating the competition.

The Pull Manufacturing focus on one production line was completing 18 units a day each and every day. A monitoring system was implemented for the purpose of collecting data from key departments every day and calculating the standard deviations, using the goal of 18 a day as the target. The standard deviation was an appropriate measure because making more than 18 received the same bad score as making less than 18. The idea was to eliminate the variance. Applying too many resources was just as bad as not applying enough resources. With the standard deviation, the only way to get a good score was to devote the right resources efficiently. At first, daily output could range from 0 to 50 units from one day to the next and varied all over the block. The end of the month hockey stick drained the production line, and it sometimes took days to get the product flowing again. The solution was as simple as demanding 18 a day, each and every day, and changing all support systems to focus on that goal. It wasn't long before everybody was talking about the "18 a day," and soon it began to happen on a regular basis.

In the period just prior to bringing in a consulting firm, this operation was running close to breakeven. Within a year after these programs were implemented, the results were wonderful! Scrap rates dropped, productivity improved, profits soared into the double digits before tax, Teams resolved manufacturing and design problems that had plagued the business for years, and the Flow Manufacturing Teams improved product flow, greatly reducing costs and dramatically improving on-time Customer delivery. But best of all, we had great fun proving that our new culture was a winner. I and others on our Team were hooked on the adrenalin derived from the continuous improvement programs and would make them our career passion. Some of these folks spent over 20 years following me from assignment to assignment and company to company, and remain zealots trying to create a better manufacturing environment at companies throughout the USA.

The lessons of these experiences are put forth here for all to see. There is really no magic, nothing very complicated, just simple concepts and ideas. Things that every manager owes himself or herself and his or her people, like continuous improvement through training and education, open and honest up front communications and employee involvement. Get outside help if you need it or do it yourself, but get going on the path to continuous improvement before it is too late.

Summary

Throughout this book I will use examples of actual real life experiences to further the reader's knowledge and understanding of successfully applying flow-manufacturing techniques in an environment of continuous improvement.

In America after World War II, most American companies were very successful and foreign competition was virtually nonexistent. There were few reasons to question the Management techniques that had been so successful for so long. Companies were very profitable and not many people were very interested in revolutionary ideas like continuous improvement or flow manufacturing. As competition from outside the USA increased, American companies began to pay a price for their high scrap rates and other inefficiencies. Pricing power began to wane, profits faltered, and some companies were forced from certain markets or, even worse, failed altogether. Out of necessity many companies have improved their performance and were able to compete with the new challenge. However, much more needs to be done by many more companies and now.

The rest of this book will be devoted to laying out a step-by-step process for taking a company from operating in the '70s or '80s mode to a very efficient and exciting company, prepared to meet and defeat the competition in the new Millennium. Topics covered will be world class continuous improvement methods such as: Lean-flow Manufacturing techniques, linked-cell manufacturing, factory Kanban, vendor Kanban, in-house store, "Bread Man routine," Wand-to-order, certified vendors, point-of-use storage, material backflushing and cross training to create flexibility. I will also cover improving competitiveness by: reducing purchase costs, low cost country sourcing, vendor pull contracts, supplier partnerships, leading in vendor negotiations and e-auctions. Also included are quality improvement techniques through Six Sigma, Statistical Process Control, Poka-yoke – mistake proofing, Out-of-Box Failure elimination, warranty expense reduction and first-pass yield improvement. Other areas of focus will include: inventory reduction, product velocity acceleration, on-time Customer delivery, floor space reduction, establishing "Cross-Functional Self-Directed" Work Teams, employee evaluation, energizing employees, and improving Union relations.

PART 2
THE FACTORY

CHAPTER 2

The Way I See It

In the new Millennium, the manufacturing companies that become "world class" will be the only companies left standing at the end of the first decade. To understand where I am coming from, we need to define "world class." A "world class" company is one that exhibits the following characteristics: The highest level of quality with yields greater than 99 percent and approaching the Six Sigma level which is 3.4 failures per million opportunities. Out-of-Box Failures, those failures your Customers experience when they first remove your product from the package and put it to use (plug it in), must be eliminated. Also, warranty expenses must be kept at their lowest possible level, usually under 1%. Lowest possible costs must be achieved through Lean-flow Manufacturing techniques and the use of the most effective tools available, such as electronic data collection systems and Kanban pull signaling methods. Keeping Customer delivery commitments will be mandatory; this means delivering product when you promised your Customer you would deliver. Closely related to keeping your delivery promise is the ability to deliver product when your Customer wants it, usually within hours or days of booking the Customer's order; this means that product throughput or velocity (the time it takes to get a finished goods item through your factory from start to finish) must be reduced to less than three days. To accomplish these initiatives Management will have to encourage real "Cross-Functional Self-Directed Teams" and empower all the available talent in the organization.

These techniques and initiatives should be employed and encouraged no matter where your products are being built. I have seen so many efforts to outsource parts, assemblies, and entire products to low cost countries and local subcontractors while forgetting to transfer lean manufacturing methods, etc. The attitude seems to be: "Oh well, we spill a little, so what? We saved a bundle by going outside or off shore." WRONG. Spill nothing. In the long run it will be just as important to your supplier or your low cost country-manufacturing arm as it is for you to optimize operations. You and your Customers will end up picking up the tab for your failure to wring every bit of waste out of your manufacturing process. Even worse, your competition executes better than you do, and first you lose your market position and maybe later your entire business.

Stay Close to Your Customer

Never let anyone get too close to your Customers. Many companies today are subcontracting final test and configuration or pick-and-pack activities to outside services companies. This can be a very big mistake. There is a definite advantage to being the last one to touch your product before your Customers do. Nobody cares as much about your Customers as you do, I don't care what arrangements you think you have with your subcontractor. Under some circumstances even the most mundane tasks should be kept at home.

The further away you get from your Customers, the less sensitive you will become to their needs. Setting your product up for your Customer and configuring the shipment is actually a form of communication with that Customer. This is where you want to be your best. To what end would you design and/or build a quality product that meets your Customer's needs at the right cost, only to hand it off to others who mishandle it, short ship key components, substitute the wrong part, choose the wrong settings during configuration, mislabel the product, under-ship, over-ship, not make a valid substitution when one is called for, or ship your product in the wrong container? Who will provide the feedback on returned shipments, make the necessary changes in carriers, or correct the packaging failures that occur? Yes, you do want to be the best at test, configuration and delivering product to your Customers.

The same criteria apply to LCCs (Low Cost Countries). If you are distributing globally from your own factories in a Low Cost Country, be sure that they are held to the same standards your USA facilities are. It often makes good sense to distribute from various regions, even if you are manufacturing in only one location. For instance, you may manufacture all of an item in the USA and distribute to the Americas from the USA, yet distribute in Europe and Africa from Germany, while Asia and Middle East distribution could be handled from Singapore. Provided all cost and logistics matters are favorable, this could be a win win for you and your Customers. Remember, I am assuming that you own the distribution centers that you are testing, configuring and shipping your product from.

This is not to say that it never makes sense to use another to distribute your product directly to your Customers. However, what it does say is that when you do, you are giving up an edge by putting someone between you and your Customer at a very critical juncture in the supplier-Customer relationship. To avoid confusion here, I am defining Customer as the individual who pays you for the product or service. This could be a distributor. In the case of the distributor you want to be the last person who touches the product before it gets shipped to that distributor. Under these circumstances, for purposes of this discussion, it is most probably not practical to ship directly to the end user, and the end user is not your Customer anyway, the distributor is your Customer – the one who pays you.

Also, when doing business with a Low Cost Country supplier, every effort should be made to get that supplier to have an in-country freight forwarder hold the supplied goods for you. You then should draw on the supply using Kanban signals in Kanban quantities that suit your requirements. Inventory ownership should take place only when you draw the material and physically take possession. A simple "letter of intent" could cover this arrangement. We will cover pull Kanban systems and letters of intent in much more detail later in this book. This method should also be used even if you own the Low Cost Country supplier. Even though you own the inventory on both ends, this will discourage abusive practices such as inventory dumping at the end of financial reporting periods to make one party look good at the expense of another. This will force your supplier, wholly owned or not, to address his inventory problems earlier. If he or she doesn't push the inventory off on his or her end, he or she will end up holding it.

Three Ways to Build

First: Work Order System

The first and in most cases the most wasteful and least desirable is the Work Order system. This system is commonly referred to as the push system. In this system an order to build is created based on some future requirement, most probably a requirements forecast. Material is then drawn from stock (kitted), staged and charged to the Work Order. Material and order are delivered to the build area where labor is applied and charged to the Order. Some companies even schedule and assign the equipment or personnel to be used with the Work Order. This is called a push system because material is pushed onto the production floor

The Way I See It

based on some forecasted requirement that will most probably change before the product is built.

There are applications where Work Orders can make sense. Say your business is such that each order you receive is truly unique in a meaningful way, and you may never receive another order for the same product. It may make sense to gather the material and charges through a Work Order. In this case, by all means use the Work Order method. Many of the tools and ideas presented here can apply to the Work Order environment. However, the pull Kanban material techniques work best when applied while working with a Lean-flow Pull Manufacturing system. See below.

In most cases Work Orders are evil. Some of my experiences are as follows: In one scenario some component is missing when the material is kitted for the Work Order. The Order is held in a kitting area until all the components are available or worse, the kit is sent to the production floor to start work. In the meantime, another order is kitted containing some of the same parts that are in the first order. Some of the components in the first order are short in the second order but present in the first order. The Shop Floor Supervisor, knowing he has a schedule to meet, robs parts from one order and applies them to another. No time to do the transaction transferring the material from one order to the next? Can't build product "A" because of parts shortages on the order? No problem, let's put up another order and maybe we will get lucky and fill it complete. By the time the order is filled more shorts – then the real robbing from one order to pay another starts. Confused yet? Don't worry, we are going to eliminate Work Orders from our manufacturing process. Imagine hundreds of orders with similar happenings. Add to the mix the charging of labor. Even the most conscientious Shop Floor Worker will end up charging his or her labor hours to the wrong order on occasion, not to mention where the careless worker could end up charging his or her time.

What do you end up with? Some unhappy Cost Accountant trying to figure out how you built 200 of product "A" without material or why it took twice as many labor hours as the standard calls for to build 200 of the same type units on another order. Ironically, some of the biggest promoters of the Work Order system are Cost Accountants, who believe they gain some measure of control with Work Orders. In reality, usually all that is gained is an out-of-control work environment. The resistance to change in this area is usually great. Historically, most Material Resource Planning systems drove companies in this direction because the systems were designed around the Work Order based system. This contributed to creating a certain comfort level that is derived from Work Orders; if you have been working with them for a long time, you feel comfortable with what is familiar. One key to a Work Order elimination program is to demonstrate to the Accountants that when you get rid of your Work Orders you greatly reduce your inventory. What better way to control inventory than to eliminate it? This is the kind of logic that appeals to the finance folks.

The following is an actual situation from one of the companies I was with; the numbers are real. In one department building sensors, work-in-process inventory was reduced from $262,000 to less than $18,000, by eliminating Work Orders. The manufacturing process had to be changed somewhat. For instance, UV cured epoxy replaced time and temperature cured epoxy. A subassembly that was done outside the plant had to be integrated into the in-house process and this required some design change and Engineering cooperation. When all was said and done, the process was converted to a Kanban pull Manufacturing system. All sensors started in production on a given day were completed and stocked within one day. The payoff was big and the Accountants wanted more of the same; once they saw the results they quickly got behind the effort.

Incidentally, there were great quality gains here also. The outside process that was being eliminated was creating a large amount of scrap and rework; the assembly, near completion, was sent to a company that was inserting the end of a delicate sensor containing infrareds, LEDs and photo diodes into a hot liquid injection molding machine. The process, which damaged and shortened the life of the sensors, was replaced with an in-house process that was done on a workbench without heat. Thus the change in the manufacturing process improved quality, and reduced scrap and rework in addition to greatly reducing inventory.

Inherent in the Work Order process is the building of inventory. The parts are brought in ahead of time and stocked, usually in a Stockroom to allow for kitting time. The kits are prepped prior to being needed on the floor to allow time for the gathering of parts shortages. The material to fill these shortages has to be expedited. When the shortages arrive, they too have to be stocked, picked and placed in the respective kits. All this putting away and picking of material takes time, therefore eating up inventory days and tying up capital.

Second: Dispatching System

The second way to build is the Dispatching system. This system is closely related to the Work Order system. It is similar in that an order to build is created, based on some future requirement, most probably a requirements forecast. The Order is then dispatched directly to the work area to await the start time and date. The big difference is that material is not drawn until work on the order is ready to begin. Material is usually pulled directly to the Shop Floor when needed, skipping the kitting stage. Although this is an improvement over the Work Order system, you are still building to a future requirements forecast. Forecasts are just that, forecasts predicting some future event that may or may not happen. Usually things do not happen exactly as forecasted.

Either you sell more or less than predicted, the product mix is off, or the timing of the sale is off. If the Customer demands and wins a feature change or Engineering issues an Engineering Change Order, you are stuck with product that has no home. This creates rework and inventory problems.

Third: Lean-flow Pull Manufacturing System

The third and most efficient way to build is the Lean-flow Pull Type Manufacturing s. In this system, you never build until the demand is present. You are not building to some future forecast that may or may not happen. You have the Customer Order in hand when you start to build or you are replenishing something a Customer just bought. A Customer Sales Order pulls finished goods off your dock. Subassemblies are pulled through the factory when a Kanban signal is given to replace material consumed in filling a Sales Order. Material is pulled onto your factory floor from your suppliers when they receive a Kanban signal given to replace material used to build a subassembly or upper-level-assembly to either fill a Customer Order or replace a subassembly or upper-level assembly that just filled a Customer Order.

Labor is charged to a product or a group of products, not to a Work Order. Labor can be monitored in one of several ways. My favorite is to collect the labor hours for a given area from time-and-attendance records used for payroll calculations. Compare this to the standard labor for the types of units completed times the number of units completed. The difference is the amount of under absorbed labor or over absorbed labor you experienced in your factory.

The Way I See It

Lean-flow Manufacturing Systems Characteristics Overview

The characteristics of a Lean-flow Manufacturing System are:

- Material flows like this: Customer Orders are pulling finished goods out of your factory; factory Kanbans are pulling assemblies through your factory; vendor Kanbans are pulling material into your factory from your vendors.
- U-shaped manufacturing cells are linked to each other and located in close proximity to the next step in the manufacturing process. If at all possible, these cells should be contiguous to the next operation in their product structure.
- Inventory flexibility and reduction are created by not committing any material to the manufacturing process until the last possible minute, while only taking ownership of inventory just before committing it to the manufacturing process and paying for the material much later.
- There are only three ways to get material into the Lean-flow Manufacturing factory:
  1. "In-house store" – your vendor maintains an inventory of parts in your factory. If there is enough business to justify it, the store is operated and maintained by an employee of your vendor. If not, you have control and are responsible to take care of and manage the vendor's inventory. Ownership of the material changes hands when you draw it from the store. This applies to both Union and non-Union environments.
  2. "Bread Man routine" – your vendor is responsible for maintaining an inventory on your Shop Floor. Parts are delivered daily to replace parts consumed in the manufacturing process. Called the "Bread Man routine"

because of its similarity to how a bread company manages the inventory of bread in a grocery store. The grocer contracts with the bread company to keep the shelves filled with fresh bread. The bread company's employees are responsible for stocking the grocer's shelves with the fresh bread and never running out of bread.

3. Vendor Kanban – your vendor delivers material in pre-arranged quantities only after receiving a Kanban signal from your Shop Floor. A Shop Floor worker breaks a minimum reserve level of inventory by drawing the inventory level down below the quantity of material deemed necessary to keep the manufacturing process going until more material can be supplied by the vendor. The smaller the Kanban quantity, the better. The signal can be communicated in one of several ways: by fax, by Internet, by phone, etc.

• Point-of-Use Material Delivery and Storage. Material is delivered to and stored where it is used. Parts used in the fabrication of products are delivered and stored in the related assembly cell. Boxes used to ship finished goods are delivered and stored in the Shipping area. NEVER STORE SO MUCH MATERIAL IN THE WORK AREA THAT YOU CAUSE THE AREA TO BECOME CLUTTERED. Either reduce the amount of material in each delivery or store the material in a warehouse. It is far better to warehouse inventory than it is to reduce efficiency on the Shop Floor because of clutter and overcrowding. One simple test is to stand up and look toward all four walls in your factory. If you can't see the North, South, East and West Walls from anywhere in your factory, you have work to do organizing your factory.

- Certified Vendors will play a key role in your Lean-flow Manufacturing facility by delivering material directly to your Shop Floor. A vendor's ability to supply material of acceptable quality must be certified under your certification program to ensure not only the consistent quality of the material they supply, but also their ability to deliver that material on-time all the time. You want the same things from your suppliers that your Customers demand from you, good quality products, delivered on time and at the lowest possible cost. Choosing suppliers who are ISO certified can save a lot of auditing time and effort, if you accept this level of independent certification as meeting your certification criteria. Of course, after the initial certification, only satisfactory performance will allow the vendors to maintain their certified status.

- No work-in-process material is present in the business. There is no need to distinguish between work-in-process material and raw material, so we can keep it in the raw material category until it is processed, assembled, packaged and stocked as a finished product. This does away with the need to transfer inventory from the raw material status to the work-in-process status, thereby eliminating all the inventory transactions and the inevitable attendant errors. Your entire factory becomes your Stockroom – for inventory transactions purposes, that is. This leaves you with only two types of inventory: raw material and finished goods. You will use backflushing to remove material from your raw material inventory. (Backflushing is the process of deducting the parts that go into a given finished goods item when the stocking transaction is performed. The transaction subtracts all the parts listed in the bill-of-material for each finished goods item transacted.) Backflushing eliminates the keying of transactions for each component used in the product being built. The only number either keyed or scanned is the finished goods number. Inventory accuracy can be maintained by cycle counting the material stocked in each work cell, based on a regular cycle counting program.

- The manufacturing elements will be clearly understood – labor, material and equipment. Given the right material, the right labor, and the right equipment, you will be able to build anything. In other words, this is all it takes to create a manufacturing operation. Combine these elements with flexibility so that you can have as many of each element as you want, whenever you want them, and you have a Lean Manufacturing operation. Sounds simple; however, this simple idea escapes many in their quest for a successful Lean Manufacturing operation.

If you are not running three shifts seven days a week, you have a given amount of flexibility with your labor. You can work overtime to increase flexibility. That is, providing the labor is properly trained.

If you are not running three shifts seven days a week, you have a given amount of flexibility with your equipment. Again, you can work overtime to increase flexibility.

Now for the hardest part, which is material flexibility. You will achieve this by mastering those techniques listed above and in the following pages.

- Training for flexibility is necessary to achieve labor flexibility. Your workforce will have to be trained and cross-trained. Promote this and talk up training until you choke on the words. Reward for the number of different jobs and tasks an employee can do. I will cover training in more detail in the pages that follow.

Customer demand pulls material into and through the factory

Again, the Customer places demand on the factory by placing an order for your finished product – filling the finished goods order causes a demand signal for the factory to build more subassemblies – building the subassemblies causes a demand signal for your vendor to deliver material. The vendor demand signal is filled in one of three ways: 1. Filled from the "in-house store," 2. Filled through the "Bread Man routine," or 3. Filled as a result of a message sent to your vendor directly from the Shop Floor (i.e., Wand-to-order via bar code – faxed Kanban signal – e-mailed Kanban signal). That is how simple it is. In this system the material you bring into your factory is in response to some Customer demand, not a reaction to some future forecast that may or may not happen.

Summary

In the new Millennium, manufacturing companies will have to become "world class" to survive. Customers will demand the highest quality at the lowest possible cost and insist on deliveries that suit their schedules. High quality levels, exceeding 99 percent levels and approaching Six Sigma (3.4 failures per million opportunities) and reduced cycle times through flow manufacturing techniques will be a must in this new manufacturing environment. Doing business in Low Cost Countries will take on new meaning. Low Cost Country producers will be held to the same standards as local companies and be forced to employ the same efficient flow manufacturing techniques to remain competitive.

There are three basic ways to build a product. First, the least desirable: The Work Order – The batch quantity to be built is based on some future forecast that may or may not materialize. The system involves kitting material, assigning the material and charging the accumulated labor to the Work Order for tracking and control purposes. Second, Dispatching system – Similar to a

Work Order in that the batch quantity to be built is based on some future forecast that may or may not materialize; however, the material is drawn directly to the Shop Floor when work on the order is to be started. Labor may or may not be charged directly to the dispatched order. Third, the most desirable method: The Lean-flow Manufacturing system – The signal to build is the result of receiving an actual Customer Order. Your Customer pulls finished goods off your dock. Assemblies are then pulled through your factory. Material is pulled onto your factory floor from your suppliers. Labor is collected by your time and attendance system.

The Lean-flow Manufacturing system exhibits the following characteristics: High throughput velocity with factory pull utilizing the In-house store, Bread Man routine and vendor Kanban techniques to acquire material; linked U-shaped manufacturing cells; low inventory levels; point of use material delivery and storage; certified vendors; fewer material transactions; a high degree of flexibility in applying the three elements of manufacturing – material, labor and equipment.

CHAPTER 3

Linked-Cell Manufacturing

All product manufactured in a Lean-flow Manufacturing facility should be manufactured in linked-cells. These cells should be contiguous to or linked in proximity and closely parallel the next operation level on the product structure. In other words, if subassembly "B" and "C" go into final assembly "A," then both subassembly "B" and "C" should be made in a cell that is in close proximity (linked) to the cell that manufactures final assembly "A." The finished goods or upper level assembly cells should be designed so that the entire product upper-level assembly can be started and completed in one cell. Material required is drawn from vendors and other nearby cells linked in the manufacturing process to the finished goods being built.

The assembly process must be clearly defined. A flow chart of the entire process will help you to understand which operations should be completed as subassemblies in feeder cells, such as circuit boards, power supplies and cable assemblies. Some tools that will be helpful in the creation of the flow chart are the bills-of-material, product structure, assembly drawings and method sheets. Remember the more work that can be done in the upper-level assembly cell, the better your flow manufacturing operation will be. The ideal situation is to do all the necessary assembly for a product and all related products in one cell.

However, this may not be practical for space, environmental, safety or other reasons. One would be hard pressed to rationalize manufacturing surface mount circuit boards in an upper-level assembly cell for a medical monitor, even though the monitor may use several circuit boards in the finished product. In this case it would probably be best to make the circuit boards in a nearby cell that made all the circuit boards for the facility. This probably would not be the case for simple cable assemblies. One could start out making cable assemblies in a feeder cell, then move toward integrating these into the upper-level cell at a later date. Or better yet, eliminate the cables from the design with connectors where practical.

Defining the Size of the Manufacturing Cell

The product size, the number of parts, volume and demand variability will dictate the cell size. I have found that for medical monitoring equipment such as cardiographs, fetal monitors, etc., 500 square foot cells are nice. One such cell was designed to manufacture 10 monitors a day. When demand doubled to 20 a day, all that was necessary was to add people to the process and the cell output was doubled. It would have been possible to redouble the output of this cell again without adding equipment or space by simply adding another shift, if necessary. This is the kind of flexibility that you should be looking to create when designing a manufacturing cell. All that said, if we were building CAT scanners, a 500 square foot cell would be far too small. Also, in the same factory I had a cell for manufacturing treadmills with four building stations. This cell was over 5,000 square feet in size. Be careful — a common mistake is to design a cell that is too large. With everything spread out, some of the benefits gained by having material and labor in close proximity are lost. One such example was defined when my Manufacturing Engineering folks moved a group of cardiographs from a sister company in another state to a manufacturing facility in Connecticut. The products were being built in a 5,000 square foot area in the sister factory. These same products were moved into a 500 square foot cell in the Connecticut facility and product costs were reduced considerably, largely through the efficiencies gained in the smaller cell.

Manufacturing Cell Output

Cell output per day, measured in terms of units per day for each cell, is a simple and useful tool that can be used to bring focus to the issue of cell output productivity. This measure will give both the cell operators and Management an idea of how the factory is performing. It will also encourage an even and smooth product flow through the factory. It is far better to be consistent with output, building, say, 10 units a day rather than building two units today and 18 units tomorrow, especially when the Customer order rate is close to 10 a day. In this scenario, on the day that the cell output is only two units, the material for the eight that did not get finished is probably back in the cell, partially built — not available to be shipped to our Customers — waste, dead inventory that could have been shipped and billed, giving us an extra day for the eight units of value on our Accounts Receivable. If we had completed and shipped the eight units that day, we would have moved them out of our inventory, and then we would get paid one day earlier for the eight units. Sounds like a little; however, if a company's annual receipts are $100,000,000 and we miss by only one day of billing a year, that is approximately $274,000 we could have in our bank account if we shipped on-time. Most companies routinely miss deliveries by far more than just one day. Measuring the cell output and insisting on consistency being one of our goals help to improve profits and deliveries, which furthers our completive position. Measuring the output with the standard deviation gives the same poor grade for manufacturing too many in a day as it does for manufacturing too few in a day. Posting the cell output with the calculated standard deviation in a highly visible place in or near the cell can be an excellent motivational tool for improving output performance. Make sure that the employees assigned to the cell are responsible for posting the data and pay attention to the numbers.

Linking Cells

All the cells should be linked by proximity to all the other cells that are feeder cells. If subassemblies are built in the same factory, their cells should be, if at all possible, contiguous with the cells they are feeding. In cases where this is not possible the material should be pulled into the consuming cell in a similar manner to the methods used in pulling material into the cell from a vendor. If duplication of equipment is necessary to maintain the integrity of our goal of building as much of the product as possible in one cell, then make every attempt to duplicate the equipment, providing the costs are not prohibitive. When figuring out these costs, be sure to take all the factors into consideration, such as the cost to carry inventory because it has to be made in batches rather than being made as it is consumed in the consuming cell. Also, don't forget the increase cost of rework and scrap when manufacturing in batches.

I like to use the two bin system for feeder cells whenever possible. In the two bin system one bin travels as the signal for replenishment (the Kanban signal) and the other bin serves as the consuming bin to be consumed in production while the traveling bin is being filled in the replenishing cell. Once the traveling bin has been filled and returned to the consuming cell, it then is ready to become a consuming bin. The cycle just keeps repeating itself. Replenishing bins become consuming bins, then they become replenishing bins again, over and over. In one actual successful factory setup, the feeder cells for subassemblies were contiguous with all the final assembly cells. The separations between the feeder and final assembly cells were a wall of wire rack carts serving as shelves. These shelves had two identical bins for each assembly used in the final assembly process. When an operator removed and emptied a bin, the full bin behind it was pulled forward, waiting to satisfy the next assembly pull. The empty bin was placed in another location, which was the signal (Kanban signal) for the feeder cell to make more of this assembly. When the empty bin was filled, it was returned to its original position, waiting for the next demand cycle. Each of the two bins contained small quantities of parts, in some cases much less than a one day supply. These subassemblies could be built quickly in the cell right next door, so why carry any extra inventory? For this process to work well, the feeder cells must be contiguous or at least close in proximity to the upper-level cells they serve. There will be more about the two-bin system to follow later in this chapter.

Communication between employees is greatly enhanced when related cells are in close proximity. Since parts and assemblies can and should be built in smaller lots in this type of manufacturing environment, the opportunity for quality feedback is excellent. Being in close proximity greatly facilitates this feedback. As soon as a defect is detected, feedback can be given from one operator in the consuming cell to another operator in the replenishing cell, thereby giving early warning of a potential problem in the manufacturing process and thus minimizing rework and preventing further defects. Also it is very helpful for all workers to understand the whole manufacturing process for a product they work on. Being closer to all the steps in the process enhances the ability to understand the entire process. The more knowledgeable employees are about the entire process, the more they will be able to contribute toward improving the process, thereby improving productivity and profitability. In one real life situation, a company suffered for years with a quality problem that went unresolved because operators were not knowledgeable about the entire build process. What was the application of too much material in one area appeared to be an oil leak in another. Units had been torn apart and reworked for years at great cost to cure what was believed to be an oil leak problem. Once the operators were educated about the entire process, the lights came on and they knew that the heat created in the testing stage was liquefying the material being applied in the earlier process. The mystery was solved, the application process corrected, and this type of oil leak disappeared, saving hundreds of thousand of dollars a year.

Designing Cells for Flexibility

It is important to design your manufacturing cells for maximum flexibility. To be flexible in serving your Customers you must create flexibility for equipment, labor and material. Equipment flexibility can be gained by working more shifts, doubling and tripling output when demand is high and/or temporary. When the increased demand cannot be satisfied by working overtime or adding shifts, equipment will have to be added, provided the payback meets the company's cost payback criteria for new investment. In some of the factories I was part of, molding was located right in the manufacturing cells, molding the parts to be consumed in the cell.

As with equipment, overtime provides flexibility for labor. My preference is to work overtime, for a long time, before the company adds people, especially if the cause for the increase in demand may be temporary. In many cases what you save in benefits by not adding people pays for the overtime premium, provided you are getting the same or better productivity in the overtime hours. Labor flexibility can also be gained through cross training. Employees should be trained to do several different jobs. This is good for the company and good employment insurance for the employees. The more different job functions an employee learns the more employable the employee becomes. Much can be gained by moving employees to areas where you have the most demand for labor. When demand slackens in one area and increases in another, you will be prepared to meet the increased demand with labor, provided you have a well cross-trained work force.

Material flexibility is gained through your Kanban pull systems. Your Kanban suppliers agree to provide you with inventory in previously agreed to quantities at previously agreed upon prices whenever you signal the supplier to deliver. The more material you need, the more frequently you will signal your supplier. Essentially your supplier has agreed to supply your material on demand. There will be much more about this to come later in this book.

The Shape of the Cell

From my experience the ideal cell configuration is the U-shaped cell. The workbenches form the sides and back of the U. I prefer manufacturing cells where the work progresses from the left to the right; it just seems more logical to me. If you have a strong preference for manufacturing cells where the work progresses from right to left, no matter, as long as you are consistent throughout your factory. The U-shape of the cell facilitates flexibility. The cell should be designed so that during slow periods one operator can perform several operations. During busy periods you can add people, to easily increase output. A good manufacturing cell design is one that will be able to at least double the cell's output during a one-shift operation. The cell's shape enhances communication between employees inside the U. You are normally closer to more of your coworkers. It is easy to just look to your left or right or even turn around to communicate on manufacturing issues with a coworker.

Cell meetings can be held right at the mouth of the U to be sure all employees are operating on the same page or to prevent and resolve problems. Short cell meetings can be held either daily or Monday, Wednesday and Friday, depending on the need, but they should be scheduled at regular intervals. The employees and the responsible supervisor should attend every meeting. In addition to the employees in the cell and the supervisor, the operators should be encouraged to ask for other support personnel to attend these meetings. For instance, a Buyer may be asked to attend, if there are parts problems or delivery issues to resolve; a Manufacturing Engineer could be requested to attend to resolve equipment problems; a Quality representative may attend to help resolve quality problems, etc. It is important that the operators in the cell be able to decide who will be requested to attend the cell meetings. Imagine the pressure on a Buyer to resolve a delivery problem, when he has to stand in front of the workers suffering because of the shortage and listen to their complaints. If the Buyer is smart, he in turn will invite the responsible vendor to attend the meeting, then watch the problem go away.

Linked-cell Kanbans

Keep in mind that the Kanban size represents the number of parts you will be pulling internally, either from another cell or from your vendor's inventory. This should be the smallest amount of material that will be necessary to sustain your operation between deliveries. If you require 10 frames a day and you have agreed with your vendor to allow two days for vendor delivery, set your Kanban quantity at a minimum of 20. If you have agreed with your vendor to take deliveries of 40 frames each time he delivers, then you set your Kanban size at 40 but you don't send a pull signal to the vendor until your on-hand inventory of frames is down to the 20 level. Be reasonable when negotiating Kanban sizes with your vendor: say a resistor comes on a reel with 5,000 pieces, they cost a penny a piece and you only use 100 a day, take the reel of 5,000 as your Kanban quantity. The point is that no formula can replace common sense.

Establishing the Kanban size is very important to the success of your pull-manufacturing program. I recommend that you keep it simple. Much has been written about how to calculate the proper size of a Kanban. Much of what has been written calls for the use of formulas to do the calculations; however, the folks that have to make the system work would be better served if they used a much simpler method. One such method I have seen successfully used in at least three implementations is simply to start with a one-week supply. This is very easy for everyone involved, including the Shop Floor workers, to understand. What you sacrifice in accuracy, you will gain ten times over in support and cooperation from your employees. They can get behind and support a system that they can easily understand, and without this cooperation you will not be successful. The one-week supply is usually much less than the on-hand inventory was in the old push system. Remember the Work Order scenario when we kitted our work orders; this usually requires a one to two-months supply of parts. So a one-week supply represents a nice inventory reduction. This is how you will sell this system to your accountant friends. After you are successfully rolling along with your program, then and only then, start a campaign to cut back on the Kanban sizes. Base your Kanban reductions on experience, not on formulas.

In one unsuccessful attempt to convert a factory from a Work Order based system to a Flow Manufacturing System, the primary reason for the failure was the detail and complexity the implementers brought to the process. After two years of effort, only one small cable product line was operating in a pull system. This amounted to less than two percent of the factory's output. The program had lost the support of the Shop Floor workers; it died and with it the entire factory. The factory was outsourced and shut down the year after the failure. Kanban pull manufacturing can be very simple, much simpler than the push work order based system. When the process is over-complicated, we lose the support of the people who cannot readily see the benefits in a complex system. The beautiful part of a pull system is that there is something in it for everyone. The Shop Floor worker's life is greatly simplified by the elimination of obvious waste. Parts shortages are eliminated, inventories are greatly lowered, profits are greatly improved, quality is improved and best of all your Customers are happier. When Customers are happy they remain loyal and buy more. All this keeps Management happy and provides for a much higher level of job security.

Kanban and the Two-Bin System

Simplify the factory with the two-bin system. Start out with two bins containing the same quantity of the same part. The bins are marked with the part number of the parts inside the bin, the Kanban quantity, the cell the parts are made in and the cell the parts are consumed in. When you empty the first bin in the consuming cell, it is returned to the cell the parts are made in. The arrival of the bin in the cell the parts are made in is the signal to build the Kanban quantity. The bin is filled and returned to the consuming cell. What could be simpler than this? No parts are built until the bin is returned to the Kanban filling cell. Material and labor are not committed until there is a real need. What a great method to allocate labor, material and equipment. Again, you can start with one week's material split between the two bins, then let experience dictate to what extent the Kanban quantity can be lowered.

Multiple Bin System: a Variation on the Two-Bin System

You can use multiple bins to set priorities within a cell. This is a variation of the two-bin system. Rather than just two bins, you can have four bins, five bins or any number of bins for that matter, containing an equal number of a part. The bins are identified as above with the part number of the parts inside the bin, the Kanban quantity, the cell the parts are made in, and the cell the parts are consumed in, and each bin is numbered sequentially. As in the two-bin system, the arrival of one of the bins in the cell the component is made in is the signal to make more. However, the number of bins that are back home in the providing cell for any given part determines the order in which the bins are to be filled. If you had five of the bins for part "X" and three of them are home, signaling a build for three bins, and you had five bins of part "Y" and all five bins were home, signaling a build for all five bins, it would be obvious that part "Y" must be built before part "X." This is a very visual system, easy to understand. Everyone in the providing cell can tell where the real priorities are.

One of my factories successfully used the multiple bin system to build sensors that were shipped with virtually every major product built and shipped from that facility. They were all manufactured in one cell. Anyone walking into the cell could just glance at the racks containing the returned Kanban boxes to determine product status. If you saw a series of bins for the same part that had five bins marked 1 of 5, 2 of 5, 3 of 5, 4 of 5, and 5 of 5 all present, you knew that item should be being built at that time. If the item was not being built, you had better find out why. This is a very defining method of allocating material and labor with a minimum of required supervision.

As with your purchased parts, it may not be practical to build 10 of an item even though you could operate with a Kanban quality of 10. If for some reason you have to build 20 at a time, then build the 20. The Kanban quantity should be 20 and the time to send the signal is when you arrive at the minimum of 10. These items are future opportunities for inventory reduction. You should constantly be in search of ways to cut your Kanban levels. One way to cut Kanban levels is to find ways to build efficiently in smaller quantities. The job of eliminating waste is never done.

Summary

Flow manufacturing should be done in U-shaped manufacturing cells that are contiguous or in close proximity to the next higher operation as defined by the product structure hierarchy. In other words, linked manufacturing cells. The cells should be designed for flexibility so that it is possible to at least double the cell's capacity in one shift by just adding people. Adding another shift will again redouble the cell's capacity. The size of the cell will be determined by the product size, volume and demand variability.

A manufacturing cell's output should be monitored and well advertised daily. Cell throughput should be prominently posted and measured with the standard deviation to demonstrate that it is equally bad to make too many, as it is to make too few in a day. The goal is a steady drum beat of output that sets the steady pace for the entire factory. A simple two-bin system or multi-bin system with bins traveling between feeder cells and consuming cells can be used to signal it is time to build more to replenish an empty bin. The empty bins' arrival in the feeder or replenishing cell is the signal to devote resources (material, labor and equipment) to build more. The multi-bin system can be used to set priorities and allocate resources – material, labor, and equipment – properly.

Communication is enhanced by the close proximity of the employees both inside the U shape of the cell and in the nearby linked cells. The product's entire manufacturing process is more easily understood as nearby related processes are made familiar to all involved in building the product. Quality issues can be quickly communicated and resolved. Regular meetings can be held in the manufacturing cell to resolve issues with all those able to contribute present. The manufacturing cell workers can request the presence of anyone they feel can assist in resolving their manufacturing issues.

CHAPTER 4

Inventory Flexibility and Reduction

One of our most important flow manufacturing goals is to create as much flexibility as possible with material, labor and equipment. Flexibility will allow us to make quick adjustments to production schedules and material requirements, giving us the ability to react to sudden changes in build plans – increases or decreases – without the necessity of keeping large stores of inventory on hand. This ability, coupled with high product throughput velocity – moving work-in-process and finished goods quickly to our Customers – will keep overall inventory at a minimum. Productivity is measured by how efficiently we use our labor, equipment and material. If we could cut all the material employed in the manufacture of goods in the USA in half, then we would be able to double the productivity of that material investment. This is a goal I hope that you will come to believe is very modest after you finish reading this book. To use an economic cliché, improving productivity raises all the boats. The added wealth generated by doubling the productivity of inventories in the entire USA would surely lead to a very dramatic improvement in the Nation's economic health.

In this chapter we will primarily deal with material flexibility. In short, always have what you need when you need it and not a minute before. On your end, you don't care when your vendor makes your parts. All you care about is that he has what you need and can get it to you when you need it.

Try to share as many of your inventory problems with your vendors as you possibly can by not taking ownership of the inventory until just before you are about to use it in your manufacturing process or ship it to your Customer. This will encourage your suppliers to come up with new solutions and methods to help you lower your inventory. The first step in this direction is to execute on the ideas previously discussed:

- The in-house stores. In this scenario your vendor owns the inventory until you draw it out of the store. Even then, you may make a payment arrangement with your vendor to pay for the goods in 60 days or more. In one of my more recent companies, the product was built, shipped, and in some cases we had even collected payment for the goods from the Customers before the vendor was paid for the material that went into manufacturing that same product. A good deal for our company; our vendors were helping to finance the operation. Similarly, Consignment inventory acts in the same manner. This is your vendor's inventory consigned to your care until you draw on it. When you use it, you notify your vendor; at that point you take ownership and the material moves into your inventory. The key difference between an in-house store and consignment inventory is that you are responsible for the care of the consignment inventory while it is in your facility. Any loss or damage is your responsibility. In an in-house store the vendor's own employees manage and keep track of their own inventory. Anything that happens to cause an inventory loss prior to your drawing the material from the in-house store is your vendor's problem, not yours.
- Next is the "Bread Man routine." Here also you can get your vendor to help you by negotiating the right deal. In

Inventory Flexibility and Reduction

one of our German operations I was helping we had negotiated an arrangement with a key vendor supplying hardware, wire and small-machined parts. As the material was removed from the vendor's designated area in our factory by our employees, a part number was entered into a PC which was integrated with a counting scale. The parts were placed on the counting scale. Each single part's weight was known by the integrated weighing system. The quantity being removed from the vendor's stock was calculated and downloaded onto a floppy disk, then the operator removed the material to the consuming area. At the end of each month, the disk was copied and one copy was forwarded to our Accounts Payable folks for payment on the negotiated date, while the second copy of the disk was sent to the vendor to be used for his inventory control system and Accounts Receivable. It was the vendor's responsibility to keep the bins in our factory that held their parts full. Obviously a certain level of trust must exist between you and your vendor for this to work. This is just one variation of the "Bread Man routine." The possibilities are virtually endless and you are only limited by your imagination. Again, using these techniques, it is easy to see how you could collect payment for products you shipped to your Customer before you have to pay your vendor for the material used in making those products.

- And lastly, we have the Shop Floor Kanbans or Wand-to-order method. Here you have very little material in your inventory, provided your vendors are delivering in small enough quantities. Hopefully, you have no more than a few days supply of parts, at least for those parts supplied by your local vendors. Here, too, you can negotiate favorable payment terms with your vendors, and again it is possible to collect payment from your Customers before you have to pay your vendors for the material that went into the product you sold your Customers.

Partnering With Your Vendors

Here is as good a place as any to talk about partnering with your vendors. It is pretty easy to take advantage of your vendor's desire to capture a nice piece of business from you, their Customer. But the relationship won't last unless there is something in it for both you and your vendor. The only good deal is a deal where both parties win.

I realize that much of what has been said so far in this book about the various methods of taking deliveries of inventory from your suppliers could sound like heavy handedness. You must always be careful to guard against this kind of behavior in your organization. If at all possible, you want to avoid even the perception of heavy handedness in dealing with your suppliers. If unfairness is allowed, you will have very short-term gains for a while, then ultimately you will fail. No vendor will tolerate being taken advantage of for any longer than he or she has to. Eventually, your prices will go up or your vendor will start to miss deliveries in favor of devoting his resources to other more profitable Customers or the quality of the material will start to slip as your vendor cuts corners in an effort to recoup some of the lost profits. Somehow you will end up paying a heavy price for taking advantage of your relationship with your vendor. Teach your Buyers and Sourcing Leaders to partner with your vendors. Insist on it! Accept nothing less than the highest ethical standards of behavior in your Sourcing group.

What follows is a real life example of a true partnership with a vendor that started out on the wrong foot. The vendor was a Wand-to-order vendor located only about 20 miles from one of our Connecticut factories. This vendor was supplying this factory over 200 different sheet metal parts on a Wand-to-order Kanban agreement covered by a "letter of intent." In an effort to convince

Inventory Flexibility and Reduction

our factory managers from Germany, who had been in the USA to learn about flow manufacturing, that Kanban agreements were effective, I sent them to visit this vendor in order to gain an understanding of the Wand-to-order process. A few years ago these ideas were quite revolutionary in Europe and as such the Germans were encountering a great deal of resistance, not only from their European vendors, but also from their own employees as well. The European vendors were flat out refusing to participate in Kanban programs and our German Management was reluctant to force these vendors with long standing relationships to comply. My intention was to convince our people in Germany that the Kanban pull system was the way of the future and they had better start moving in this direction or be left behind.

They were impressed all right. Our vendor showed them a warehouse full of our parts that they were storing for us. Not exactly what I was hoping for. The German representatives thought it was great that we could force our vendors to hold our inventory. I was not at all impressed with the huge stores of material waiting for a Kanban signal from our Factory Floor. I realized that this vendor had continued to manufacture our parts in the same old way as he had prior to getting on board with the Wand-to-order program. It didn't take a rocket scientist to figure out that it would only be a question of time before this vendor would come to resent financing our company by keeping parts he had manufactured for us on his books. Then a good vendor relationship would go bad. He would try to find a way to recoup his lost profits at our expense.

I had to explain to my German friends that the concept of the Kanban pull systems could and should be a two way street. It should be a good deal for their vendors, as well as a good deal for them. I assured them that the intent of the Kanban pull system was not just to get their vendors to hold their inventory but to improve the efficiency and profitability of both companies. The vendors should be using the same techniques to minimize their inventory and material investment as we were. They do this by improving their throughput velocity and changing their manufacturing methods so that they can react quickly to changes in our demand. Also, in turn the vendor should be working with his suppliers, encouraging them to deliver material on a demand-pull basis. After our German friends left for home, we had to take action to fix our own problems with this favored vendor, while the relationship was still in good shape and could be salvaged.

The remedial action took place over the next several months and further cemented an excellent working relationship with a healthy, prosperous supplier that would work with us for years to come. The first step was bringing the vendor and several of his people to our facility for training. The next step was to offer our vendor the services of one of our Manufacturing Engineers, who had many years of experience in manufacturing products similar to the ones they were supplying us. The deal was, we pay for the Manufacturing Engineer and we split 50/50 any cost savings generated as a result of the effort. They accepted, realizing they could improve their overall competitive position by applying the same techniques to their other Customers' parts. After several months of devoting either one or two days a week working together in our vendor's shop, several manufacturing methods and equipment changes were made. A laser cutter was added, which greatly increased flexibility. Where necessary, blanks were cut and kept in stock instead of finished goods. The blanks could be quickly turned into finished parts when needed. Our Engineers working with their engineers made several design changes, which made the parts easier and quicker to manufacture. This included switching to common hardware so that fewer part numbers were required to make the same end items. The vast majority of these changes were minor, and many led to better and more robust designs. And to top it all off, we were able to gain some nice cost savings that far exceeded the cost of our

Inventory Flexibility and Reduction

investment in this long- lasting relationship with this vendor. Truly a win win situation for all involved.

On another occasion with a not so happy ending, we were doing business with a local vendor who was manufacturing wooden cabinets that we sold as a third party item with our equipment. The cabinets were offered more to please our Customers' desire for one stop shopping than to produce profits. They were being sold for close to cost, around $400. This local vendor refused to deliver on a demand-pull basis, claiming he was a small operation and needed to deliver when the cabinets were finished, no matter what the requested delivery date was. After several attempts to work with this vendor failed, my Sourcing Manager started looking for another source of supply. The search, that was initiated in an attempt to find a vendor that would deliver on a demand-pull basis, also yielded a cost savings of around 30%, making this product now profitable. One problem, the vendor was not local. He was located in the Midwest. My Sourcing Manager and my Logistics Manager worked out a great deal with this Midwest supplier whereby the supplier would drop ship directly to our Customer upon receipt of a faxed copy of one of our Customer Orders. After the supplier trained their employees to fill our Customers' Orders, this process worked well for years.

The local vendor we had been using was devastated. They had believed that our many protests of the way they did business were just so many attempts to squeeze them for price reductions and get them to hold our inventory. We brought them in and laid out the new deal we had with our new vendor in the Midwest. They admitted to us, and more importantly to themselves, that because of the way they currently ran their business, they could not have matched the deal even if they had taken us at our word that we would have to find another vendor to replace them. They had to change or go out of business. The story does not end here.

Winning in a Highly Competitive Manufacturing Environment

A few months later I happened to be in the Midwest and decided to call on this vendor to see how they were doing with our carts. We had given them a large blanket order for 1,200 carts. Our history showed that the sales for these carts were pretty linear. We averaged five a day; some days we may have shipped none, other days we could ship 10 or even 15, but almost never would we ship more than 15. When we went for a tour of their shop, they were pleased as punch to show us the 400 carts they had nearing completion and further boasted about the material they had on hand for the next 400 carts. I was stunned. He could have built the carts very efficiently in lots of 25. Then the Owner of this privately owned company showed me his warehouse with well over a million dollars of material in stock, mostly readily available lumber. I knew that to be able to maintain a successful and long-lasting relationship with this supplier, we had to help him understand more about inventory Management.

I started by asking him if there were great quantity discounts for the lumber he bought. There were, but they were not significant enough to justify the carrying cost. I asked if he thought he could get his suppliers to accept large orders at the prices he was currently paying, but deliver and bill on short notice. He was sure he could arrange this. Then I next asked him if he would like an extra million dollars in his bank account. The light came on. I assigned a Sourcing Manager to work with his company, educating them on pull manufacturing techniques. This Supplier went on to serve us well over the next several years, delivering cost reductions and performing further added value services. This relationship made our company a lot of money on cart sales in the following years, an item we had carried and sold at close to breakeven just to satisfy the one stop shopping demands of a few Customers. Another win win for all.

On occasion, for the good of all parties involved, you do need to be forceful in your relationship with your vendors. When necessary, this should be done with the purest of motives. You can

Inventory Flexibility and Reduction

hardly ever go too far wrong when you are being aggressive with your vendor for the right reasons, as in the case of assisting our German manufacturing arm with their vendors. Eventually the vast majority of their vendors were convinced to deliver goods based on some form of a Kanban pull system. Although they were resistant at first, they came to realize (with a push from the US side) that they could use these techniques as a competitive advantage by offering the same services to other Customers. Members of our US Sourcing Team spent weeks in Europe visiting vendors with our local Sourcing Manager and putting it on the line – get on board or we will be forced to shop elsewhere. Once they got on the bandwagon, it wasn't long before they were coming up with unique ways to deliver material, based on their own version of the Kanban pull system.

One German sheet metal vendor, located a block away from our factory there, started an in-house store with over 300 different sheet metal parts in stock, located just off of our Shop Floor. Another did the same with manuals. Yet another introduced the "Bread Man routine" with hardware, carrying the concept one step further by adding machined parts. And another vendor supplied raw cable the same way. Wand-to-order was successfully introduced with suppliers for circuit board and electronic components. Packaging material such as cardboard shipping boxes were delivered on a Wand-to-order basis. Computer hardware was also delivered based on the Wand-to-order system. It did not take long to turn these skeptics into zealots. What had been believed to be impossible by our German Operations folks just a year earlier was now their standard operating procedure, and they were proud of their revolutionary systems. Before long, other German companies, seeking advice about how to replicate these successful operating systems, were regularly visiting this German factory to learn what they could about Kanban flow manufacturing. It was not long before our German colleagues were improving on what we had taught them and in turn were sharing their new ideas with our people back in the USA.

Velocity

Velocity, how long it takes to manufacture and move product through your factory, is every bit as important as the methods used to bring material into your facility. If you have enough material in your factory to build a month's supply of a particular finished product and it takes a month to build the product with all the material present, then you are turning that inventory 12 times a year. You are getting 12 turns on those committed assets. One way to double your turns on these inventory assets is to cut your cycle time in half, or, to put it another way, increase your velocity to two weeks for this product and its attendant material and this will then give you 26 turns annually. Better yet, improve your processes so that the cycle time is reduced to one week and you will be at 52 turns a year. Nice improvement and your material assets for this product are now more than four times as productive as they were when you started with a turn of 12. This is a very achievable and worthy goal.

Improvement in velocity starts when you start to measure it. Most companies don't even know what their throughput velocity is. Remember our previous conversation about sensor cycle time in Chapter 2. This sensor producing department in one of my factories was able to reduce inventory from $262,000 to less than $18,000 by converting their manufacturing system from a Work Order push system to a Kanban pull system and changing some of their methods of manufacturing. In this instance the methods changes included: 1. Converting to UV cured epoxies, eliminating the time and temperature curing wait time. 2. Bringing part of the process in-house that had previously been outsourced to eliminate the vendor's operation time, queue time and the travel time to and from the outside vendor. These actions resulted in a better than 93% reduction in inventory. Some of

Inventory Flexibility and Reduction

these sensors, prior to the changes, used to remain in process for as long as six weeks. After the changes to a Kanban pull system and the assembly methods changes, all sensors were completed in no longer than eight hours. We will talk much more about velocity in future chapters.

Dealing With Low Cost Country (LCC) Suppliers

Another important consideration when dealing with very long supply chains such as Low Cost Country Suppliers in places such as China, India, and Eastern Europe, is the amount of safety stock you need to carry. The types of issues that must be taken into consideration are missed or cancelled flights, other shipping delays, Customs clearance time, Government agency inspections, holidays, etc. Every attempt should be made to move the responsibility for controlling these issues to your Low Cost Country suppliers. One answer is to have your LCC suppliers contract with a freight forwarder located near your operation to deal with importing, clearance and warehousing issues. Then the material can be pulled into your operation with a Kanban signal. Under these circumstances your Low Cost Country supplier takes the responsibility for carrying the necessary safety stock. In this way the supplier will be highly motivated to execute well on his end to avoid problems on your end, making the safety stock requirement minimal. After all, your supplier has more control over the supply chain than you do, and it makes sense for the one with the most control to have the most responsibility in getting the goods to you when you need them.

Other Inventory Reducing Considerations

There are many other inventory reducing ideas that should at least be considered in any good inventory reduction program. A few of my favorites are covered below:

- Reducing the part numbers that go into building your products. Manufacturing Engineering should be scrutinizing every new release to find parts that can be replaced with parts already called out on other existing products. Don't forget to mine existing designs for part elimination prospects. Changing to common hardware, common material thickness or common electronic components will often have no effect on product aesthetics or quality. Educating design engineers to be sensitive to these issues will go a long way toward stopping unnecessary proliferation of part numbers. Also, consider adding a change control process that forces engineers to scrutinize existing parts availability before releasing a new part.

- Kanban size reduction. Kanbans should be constantly reviewed for ways to reduce Kanban size. There should be an annual reduction goal established that Operations and Sourcing Leaders commit to.

- Never accept early deliveries. It does not take long to train your vendors to refrain from unauthorized early delivery. Most business systems can identify and reject early shipments on receipt. You have two ways to deal effectively with this problem. The first is to refuse all early shipments. The second is to accept the early shipment and hold the payment while communicating with the vendor that his payment will be held because of his early delivery.

- Expedite material to be returned to your vendors (RTV material). Busy buyers tend to let these issues slide. This area always seems to be a problem. Measure your buyers on how quickly they deal with these issues. A very visible designated area labeled with the responsible Buyer's name will also help manage this issue. Make sure each person involved in the process understands that this material is on your books while it is on your property.

- Coordinate new product introductions very carefully with the Marketing and Sales organizations. If your Sales organization starts to take orders for the new product before material unique to the old product is consumed, you will be stuck with obsolete goods. Also, Sales personnel must be careful about the timing of announcements for the release of a new product. If they announce too early, Customers may wait to buy and again you will be stuck with material for the old product. Again, education is the key here. Educate those involved with new product introductions, giving them a clear understanding of the impact on inventory, especially how this can affect future product costs which will result in increasing their Customer's prices, making your products less competitive.

- Be very careful how you recognize the value of returned goods. Make sure you don't take them back into your inventory at a value greater than you can resell them for. If you are taking a worthless piece of equipment back in trade on a new sale, write it off on return. Better yet, identify and write it off as a discount on the sale – that is what it really is — and be sure and reduce the Sales commission by the value of the worthless returned goods. Don't pay taxes on false earnings in one period only to have to write off the returned goods in another financial period; you will just be kidding yourself, and soon you won't be able to tell what segments of your business are profitable and which ones are not. You need to understand the effects of your inventory decisions on your operation's profitability. Another caution: don't pay Sales commissions for goods that are returned when a Customer decides not to keep the product. This will only encourage more borderline sales that don't stick.

- Control your demo inventory closely. Keep your demo inventory turning over. If at all possible, have your Sales people sell their demo equipment in the field, turning it over often. It is usually far better to sell your demo equipment at a deep discount than to write it off because it is too old to sell. Caution: be on the lookout for demo equipment that has turned into a gift. Analyze the age and whereabouts of your demo equipment to unveil product that is carried as demo, but has been really out on a long-term loan or even gifted – sanctioned or not. This equipment should be dealt with, either billed for or expensed.

- Fire sale obsolete product early or off load it to a used equipment dealer. The earlier you deal with it, the bigger the return will be. Few manufactured products increase in value when they age unless they reach antique status. Unless you are in the antique business, make time to deal with these issues early. Write it off, gift it to schools and take the tax deduction to lower your taxes.

- And finally, outsourcing entire assemblies eliminates the need for the entire inventory that goes into making the assembly in-house. Any item that is not part of your core competency should be considered for outsourcing. Be careful here; do not outsource items that will increase your product cycle time.

Summary

Creating flexibility in your flow manufacturing facility will be one of your strongest weapons in your fight to reduce your inventory investment. The productivity of these inventory assets will greatly affect your profitability. Cut your inventory in half and you will double the productivity of your inventory assets. Our three favorite methods of acquiring material will be valuable tools in our inventory reduction efforts; they are the in-house store, the "Bread Man routine," and the vendor Kanbans or "Wand-to-order" methods.

Inventory Flexibility and Reduction

Partnering with your vendors is essential for a successful inventory reduction program. Only by dealing fairly with your vendors will you gain their support and help in achieving your goals. It is hard to imagine a successful inventory Management program without the support of the vendors involved. Cultivate these relationships even if it means that you have to help your suppliers manage their operations. You should share in your vendor's cost savings that result from these joint efforts.

Velocity — how long it takes to manufacture and move product through your factory — is every bit as important to inventory Management as the methods used to bring material into your facility. If you double the velocity of the material in your factory, that material will be present for half the time, doubling its productivity or reducing your inventory asset investment by half.

There are many other inventory reducing considerations, including: the proliferation of part numbers; Kanban size; early deliveries; RTV material; new product introductions; recognition of returned goods; demo inventory; obsolete goods and outsourcing products or assemblies.

CHAPTER 5

Velocity

When I use the term velocity, I am referring to the speed at which you can move a product through your factory from start to finish. The clock starts ticking as soon as you take the first action to build any part of the product. If your product contains circuit boards, and you populate them in your facility with your own equipment and your own people, the product is started when you put the first component on the fab or raw board, provided the circuit board is the assembly that is started first. If your product contains another assembly that would have been started prior to the circuit board, then the moment you started that assembly is the moment your end product was started. If you buy your circuit boards complete on a turnkey basis, you don't count the time it takes your subcontractor to build the board for your product. However, if you are kitting the material and supplying it to a vendor to build circuit boards for you or any other assembly for that matter, then you should count the time from the day you start the kitting process. The clock stops ticking the instant the product is stocked as a finished goods item.

For most businesses, cycle time will be measured in terms of days or fractions of a day. If you already have cycle times that you are measuring in terms of minutes, you are probably wasting your time reading this section. I encourage you to go do something more productive with your time.

Converting from push to pull will have a dramatic effect on your cycle time. In a push manufacturing system the cycle time clock starts ticking when you start putting together the first kit for any part of the product. For a flow-manufactured product there is no need to put a kit of material together, so you skip the process altogether and whatever kitting time there would have been is saved. I refer again to the example of the sensor assembly department in one of my former companies. In this example we converted from a push manufacturing system to a pull manufacturing system using flow-manufacturing techniques, as well as bringing inside subassemblies previously outsourced and modifying some assembly procedures. We were able to reduce product cycle time from six weeks to one day (one shift). This had a great effect on WIP inventory, reducing it from $262,000 to $18,000. As you can see from this example, cycle time and inventory are closely related.

In one of my more recent factories, where we were manufacturing very sophisticated medical equipment as well as the sterile disposable products that were used with the equipment, we were able to reduce cycle time from 14 weeks to three days. This equipment and the facility manufacturing it fell under the Food and Drug Administration's scrutiny. Their "Good Manufacturing Practices" were strictly adhered to. Some of the products we manufactured in this facility were considered "class three devices." This meant components that were considered critical had to be traceable back to the manufacture and forward to each piece of equipment the components were installed in. Many of the products had more than ten circuit boards and many of these were populated and tested in this facility. So you can see it was no cakewalk to get to a cycle time of three days or less. It took the "Cross-Functional Self-Directed Work Team" over a year to reach their three-day target. We will talk more about "Cross-Functional Self-Directed Teams" later in this book.

The Team that led the cycle time reduction effort was composed of members from different functions in the business, in other words, a Cross-Functional Team. Manufacturing was of course present. They had the most to gain and provided the leadership. Manufacturing Engineering representatives were deeply involved with new methods, tooling changes, factory layout, and test procedure improvements. Manufacturing Engineering is a great area to drive change from in your manufacturing business. They are skilled at finding and applying new methods that lead to adapting new and enlightened manufacturing techniques. Quality Assurance was very instrumental in burn-in time reduction and other testing improvements that would ring time out of our processes, while maintaining the highest level of quality. Materials Services concentrated their efforts on point of use storage, improved material flow and transaction elimination. Although each Team member was picked for his or her particular expertise, every Team member was expected to make contributions in all the other areas that involved cycle time as well, and they did. One of the advantages of using a "Cross-Functional Team" to solve a problem like this is that you have many new people whose vision is not clouded by the prejudices caused by looking at the same old problem for a long time. People with a fresh look tend to see things that those who have been living with the problem for years can no longer see. As a result, they can more easily think out of the box.

Data Collection

As I have said before, "Improvement in velocity starts when you start to measure it." Most companies don't even know what their throughput velocity is because they have never bothered to measure it. The data collection mechanism you select should be simple to understand and the data easy to collect, automatically, if at all possible. Data collection is best accomplished with an automated data collection system. In one of my companies, at the time a product was moved to final stock, the stocking transaction for moving the product to finished goods inventory took place concurrently with the transaction to backflush the material that went into building the product. Simultaneously, the system calculated time and date the circuit boards were birthed. (This was the moment that a circuit board was assigned a bar code at the start of the circuit board assembly process.) The circuit board was always the product component with the longest cycle time – the subassembly that had been started first. Also, the system knew the bar code of the circuit boards in each finished goods item for quality tracking purposes. Violà, you have the start time and the end time. The time in between is your cycle time. You can calculate your cycle time in actual days, including weekends and holidays, or in workdays. Calculating cycle time in workdays is by far the preferred method. Including weekends and holidays only confuses the issue by mixing product built and completed without weekends or holidays with product built that included weekends and/or holidays in their cycle time calculations.

An automated data collection system will communicate with your business system and greatly assist in managing your entire business. An automated data collection system will allow you to use bar code scanners to send Kanban signals both inside your facility and to your vendors outside your facility. You will be able to backflush inventory as product is transacted to finished goods, eliminating thousands of transactions and their inevitable transaction errors. The system will help you track, collect and perform Pareto analysis of failure data to better understand quality issues that will lead to improved quality. You will be able to set failure parameters so that when you have more than one failure of the same type in the same day anywhere in your factory, it will automatically send a warning signal to the members of your First Pass Yield Team so they can analyze and fix problems in the early

Velocity

stages. Receiving and shipping product can be automated, eliminating manual transactions and errors. If you are manufacturing a regulated product that you must keep track of by serial number, an automated system is a must, especially if you need to maintain product history files to be used in the event of a product recall where regulators virtually leave no room for error.

In the absence of an automated system, keep the manual system you design simple. It can be as simple as a manufacturing document that contains a record of the start dates for the subassemblies and finished product, and travels with the product through your factory. Collecting these data sheets and keying them into a spreadsheet will provide the information needed to calculate your cycle time. You should consider not only the average cycle time, but also the range of throughput time. You will want to pay special attention to those units that seem to get stuck in your system for long periods of time. Examining the causes of these delaying problems can lead to solutions, which eliminate the outliers that skew your data, making your numbers worse than they need to be.

Solving Material Flow Problems

Poor material flow will greatly increase your cycle time. Parts shortages can slow the process down by weeks. It only takes one missing part to hold up an entire unit. Your inventory sits idle in your factory while your product cycle time grows and grows. The causes of these problems are many; the solutions are usually simple. These problems can result from unreasonable Customer delivery promises by Sales or Order Entry personnel; errors in the planning process – often in the business system bills-of-material or the product structure; late Purchase Orders caused by cumbersome ordering systems that require full blown Material Requirements Planning runs before parts can be ordered; poor vendor performance, usually associated either with your planning system or the lack of a certified vendor program; obsolete components used for manufacturing your older designs that should be considered for obsolescence; poor vendor quality caused either by poor design or the absence of a vendor certification program; lost components – point of use storage will solve many of these problems; high scrap rates, and more. The causes are many; the fix is to be found in a linked-cell flow-manufacturing system and the practices and method that accompany that system.

I had just started in a new position running a factory with output of around $100,000,000 a year, manufacturing medical equipment. The Purchasing Manager had resigned a few weeks before I arrived. I hired a great Purchasing Manager, whom I had worked with for 10 years at a previous employer. Our start dates with this new company were only days apart. I requested that we review each of the purchase requisitions entering his department that did not allow enough lead time to effectively acquire the material. We thought this would reveal any problems with poor Customer commitments and the material planning system. My new Purchasing Manager returned several hours later with a green bar report that was over 10 inches thick in both of his outstretched hands. He said, "Ron, you asked me to review all the requisitions that don't allow us enough lead time to purchase material." "Right," I said. He then continued, "You don't really mean that – here they are and they all have request delivery dates prior to the day the requisitions were released to Purchasing." There were 867 parts shortages on the Shop Floor at that point in time. We had a major manufacturing systems problem and I knew I would be adding another employee from my past to help us fix these problems — I did and he did.

This turned out to be one of the best factories my Team had ever fixed. After the implementation of a Kanban pull manufacturing system, cycle time went from 14 weeks to less than three days. At the same time, parts shortages went from 867 parts shortages that were weeks old to a handful that were solved in a few days. Employee morale skyrocketed. One of the most stressful situations a production worker can find himself or herself in is one where they are constantly fighting parts shortages, especially when they are the same ones over and over, as they tend to be. Inventory dropped from $24,000,000 to $7,000,000 during the implementation period for the Lean-flow Manufacturing System we implemented. At the same time, cycle time improved to less than 3 days.

There are two important lessons that should not be missed in the above situation. First, more material is not the solution to a shortage problem. With $24,000,000 of inventory, there were 867 parts shortages, and with $7,000,000 in inventory, there were virtually no parts shortages. Simply, the $7,000,000 of inventory was the right inventory. Second, if this factory had been operating with a pull Kanban material system, even a broken material requirements planning system could not have caused enough chaos to create 867 parts shortages. Why? Because in a pull Kanban system, you do not rely on your planning system to determine when you order material. Your Kanban signal tells your vendors when to deliver, based on real requirements – a Customer demand. The only thing you ask from your material requirements planning system is that it project future requirements so that your vendors have an idea of what you will be demanding. Most suppliers use their own experience and then pad it a little. Further, if they are smart, they are running their shop like you are and can react rapidly to your changes in requirements anyway.

Changes in Manufacturing Methods

Changing the way you manufacture your products will have as much of an impact on your cycle time as changing your material flow. Each process must be reviewed to eliminate time – be it queue time, travel time, set-up-time, cure time, burn time or process time. Mine each of these areas for time reduction opportunities. Review each opportunity, pick the low hanging fruit and then repeat the process over and over. These are fun projects that generate confidence and excitement for your employees. They are excellent candidates for Six Sigma projects. The successes are easily measurable and each success should be celebrated. I can taste the pizza.

Review each cell for set up. Add equipment wherever practical. Bring processes done outside the cell, inside the cell. Make sure feeder cells are contiguous with consuming cells. Point of use inventory supplies should be readily available and easily accessible to all who use them. Ergonomics should be reviewed. Make adjustments to cell layout if necessary. Use (mistake proofing) techniques to eliminate errors and speedup the assembly and test processes.

Adding equipment can be a very effective method of reducing cycle time. We have added ultrasonic welders to cells, eliminating the need for parts to travel halfway across the factory from one department to another that had an ultrasonic welder used in a different manufacturing cell for another application. This eliminated the need for the welded assembly to be made in batches, making rejects immediately detectable, because the parts were consumed in the next operation right after they were welded. Also, set up time was eliminated on both welders. The new welder could be devoted to the parts being consumed in its cell and the old welder could be devoted to parts used in its cell. Also, the two welders could act as backup for each other in the event of a breakdown. Do your cost analysis here to justify the addition of new equipment, but don't forget to take all the cost saving benefits into consideration.

In another cell we added an inkpad printer. The ink used was quick drying, so that the parts could be used right after the printing was done. This single piece of equipment knocked days out of the overall process. Prior to our adding this equipment to the cell, the parts were sent to an outside ink stamping facility in the

Velocity

next State. Bringing the ink stamping inside removed at least a week from the entire process.

Changing circuit board assembly equipment can greatly reduce your cycle time. Although most products are now using surface mount boards (circuit boards with components glued and soldered to the surface of the board) rather than through-hole boards (boards with components that have leads that go through the boards), they are an excellent example of how equipment change can speed up your process. Highly automated surface mount equipment can place as many as 15,000 to 20,000 components an hour. The through-hole technology we had in my last facility that manufactured through-hole boards could place little more than one thousand components an hour.

If you are stuck manufacturing through-hole boards, the assembly equipment can be greatly improved upon. Random component locators that indicate where the operator should place the next component can be synchronized with an automated bin system that rotates to the bin containing the next component. Small lots of boards can be populated efficiently with this equipment when it is automated so that the operators can key in the board type they are making, and only the correct bins for that board are displayed with the location indicated in the correct sequence.

Improving or adding test equipment can be very productive. Test equipment can download and archive test results automatically, eliminating the need for operator record keeping. Involve your operators here. Ask them to help design tests that will be mistake-proof solutions. This is one area where you want to do your best. Whether you are testing your product to screen out failures, or filling a regulatory requirement, this is probably the last time you will see your product perform before the Customer does.

We asked our employees in the final configuration and test cell to help us solve a problem with a monitor we were building. The monitor would arrive at the last bench of the cell ready for final configuration and test. At this point the operator would refer to the build list to determine what language and communication features this unit should receive. Next the software was downloaded and the communication features added. It was also necessary to manually set the DIP switches inside the unit in the correct position. Every once in a while these units would be returned from the field because the operator failed to set the DIP switches in the correct position. The solution designed and implemented by the Team in the cell was to change the software so that the final unit test could not be completed or downloaded until the DIP switches were set as indicated by the software that was downloaded to the unit. Sounds simple and obvious, and it was, as are most of the best solutions to manufacturing problems.

In the sensor-manufacturing cell referred to above, changes in the type of epoxy were significant contributors to cycle time improvement. Epoxies that are cured with an ultraviolet light replaced time and temperature epoxies that had to stand over night to cure. UV cured epoxy allows the operator to cure the epoxy immediately after application with a hand-held ultraviolet light. The assembly process can continue without the need to rack, stack and wait for the assembly to cure. This eliminates many touches as well as removing the curing queue time from the cycle time. We also were able to purchase the epoxies premixed from the manufacturer. Buying them premixed eliminated the variability in the in-house mixing operation. You can buy many types of epoxies premixed, packed in dry ice and shipped overnight. Usually this is an insignificant part of your product cost, and the increased cost to buy premixed material is usually well worth the elimination of the variations in the mixing process. It also eliminates a job almost nobody likes.

Many products containing sensitive electronics require a burn-in period. This is operating your product either at elevated or ambient temperatures for a specified period of time, usually for the purposes of early failure detection and elimination.

Elevating the temperature can usually speed up the process. Also, the circuit boards may be burned in on a simulator prior to assembly. Burning-in just the boards eliminates the need for tying up the entire assembly at the end of the line when it carries the highest value. However, the best way to cut burn-in time is to eliminate it.

Great care must be exercised here. We never want to compromise product quality for the sake of decreasing cycle time. This is when you need the cooperation and assistance of your Quality Assurance and Engineering Teams. In one of my companies we formed a separate Burn-in Reduction Team to carefully address these issues. Manufacturing Engineering took the lead. We sent Manufacturing Engineers and Quality Engineers to take a course at a Midwestern University specifically designed for Burn-in time reduction and elimination. They would become the technical resources for the Team effort. If you are manufacturing medical equipment or Government equipment, you cannot just reduce your burn-in-time without consideration and proof of the burn-in-time reductions' effect on the products' efficacy. The reduction must be backed-up by statistical evidence justifying your actions. In this company the Team was able to eliminate over 90% of the burn-in time. In some cases electronic components had to be replaced with more robust components. The effort paid off big. Burn-in was completely eliminated for several products that had exceeded 48 hours and remaining burn-ins on other products were drastically reduced. In many other product burn-ins we were burning-in at the board level as well as the finished unit level. In these cases we were able to eliminate one or both of the burn-ins, removing as much as 96 hours per unit from the process.

Cycle time reduction will have a very positive effect on your inventory investment as well as greatly improve your Customer response time. Imagine only needing three days of work in process material to cycle product through your facility in three days when you once needed a 14-week supply of work in process material to cycle product through your facility in 14 weeks. Talk about material productivity. This kind of productivity improvement is real. If you don't believe it and take action soon, your competition will, and that competition may be in Asia someplace.

Summary

Velocity is the speed at which you can move a product through your factory from start to finish. To measure velocity, start at the instant the first action is taken to build the first assembly that makes up the product and stop when the finished product is stocked. The time in between the start and finish is the cycle time or throughput velocity. Converting from a push to a pull manufacturing system will have a dramatic effect on your cycle time.

Improvement in velocity starts when you start to measure it. The data collection system you select should be simple. An automated system would work best; however, a simple manual system such as a document that travels with the product from start to finish, documenting the start time and date as well as the completion time and date, will do the trick.

Solving material flow problems will greatly increase cycle time. Linked-cell flow manufacturing can resolve the following material flow issues: parts shortages; unreasonable Customer delivery promises; planning process errors; late Purchase Orders; late vendors' deliveries; lost components and high scrap. More material is not the solution to your material flow problems, but the right material is.

Changing the way you manufacture your products will have as much impact on your cycle time as changing your material flow. Mine your processes for time elimination opportunities. Eliminate or reduce queue time, travel time, set up time, cure time, burn-in time, and process time. Review your

Velocity

manufacturing cell setups. Add equipment when necessary. Mistake-proof your processes. Bring outside processes inside when necessary. Reduce burn-in time.

Increasing your velocity or reducing your cycle time will lower your inventory investment and improve your profits and your Customer deliveries. It can also have a positive effect on quality.

CHAPTER 6

The In-house Store

In this chapter we will discuss in detail the concept of the in-house store. With the in-house store your company provides a vendor with a designated area to maintain a store where he can stock and distribute items that he sells your company. This area is usually a secured area. You own the fixtures and your vendor owns the material. The Store Keeper is paid by and is an employee of the vendor. The Store Keeper's function is to maintain the stock in the store and distribute the items to your employees or the consuming area when signaled to do so by your employees. This would include receiving material from the vendor's warehouse, stocking the material in a location in the in-house store and issuing the material to your workers in one of several ways. The vendor's Store Keeper would be responsible for taking inventories in the store and maintaining records of transactions and inventory balances for the vendor. This does not have to be a full time position. If the level of business requires two hours a day, then the Store Keeper only need be in the store for the two hours a day. However, you do need to have access to the store during the hours you do not have coverage. A trusted employee in your organization can hold the key. This is usually the Buyer responsible for establishing and managing the relationship with the vendor. The Buyer has a vested interest in seeing that any necessary paperwork to cover off-hour withdrawals is done correctly.

Your arrangement with your in-house store vendor may include delivering material directly to the work cell or even the bin in the work cell. The arrangement may call for the Store Keeper to simply place the material on racks outside the store with the area the material is designated for marked clearly on the material. You can use any one of several Kanban signals to signal a delivery request. If you have an automated data collection system with scanners, the Kanban card can be scanned to send the Kanban signal directly to the in-house store. In the absence of an automated system, Kanban cards can be dropped in a bin outside the store and collected once a day by the Store Keeper. Also, the Store Keeper can have access to your business system and collect delivery signals directly from your system at prearranged intervals.

A red warning flag must be raised for any request for material that cannot be filled immediately. The contracting Buyer should be notified as soon as possible. This had better be a very infrequent occurrence. After all, the purpose of the in-house store is to create material flexibility. The agreement with the vendor should clearly state that the vendor must have what you want, when you want it, provided the item is covered in the contract. Agreed-on parameters should be covered in your formal agreement with the vendor.

The Agreement

The agreement should cover:
- The part numbers the vendor will stock.
- The price you will pay for each part.
- The "letter of intent," if there is one.
- How often you will quote the operation to the competition – usually no more often than once a year.

The In-house Store

- How the quote will be constructed (usually you will insist that the vendor sell you the material in the in-house store at a price equal to or lower than you can buy it elsewhere. You must be reasonable here. By reasonable I mean allowing comparisons based on a basket of parts. Your vendor may lose because he is a penny higher on a resistor; however, he may be 4 pennies cheaper on two other resistors. Switching in-house store vendors is a lot of work and very costly. Don't change vendors for a few cents.
- Actions the vendor is expected to take when his normal supply of material is interrupted.
  - Who bears the extra cost to buy the parts elsewhere or the design costs to redesign another replacement part into your product?
  - Process for obtaining permission to substitute material.
  - Proper notification procedures for substituted material.
- Separation agreement.
- Designated space.
- Access to your facility.
- Hours of coverage.
- How much material the vendor is expected to be able to supply, i.e., 120% over your normal usage as reflected in your Material Requirements Planning monthly requirements report.
- How you will communicate future requirements to your supplier.

Transaction Simplification

There are plenty of opportunities to simplify the business transaction for removing material from the in-house store. This can be done electronically, setting up the Accounts Receivable for the vendor and Accounts Payable for you automatically when material is transacted out of the store. The transaction can also transfer the material into your inventory automatically at the same time. The material can then be transacted out of your inventory when the finished goods item is transacted to final stock, using the "backflushing" method based on your bills-of-materials. With this system, virtually all your material movement transactions are done electronically, eliminating the hundreds of errors normally created when thousands of items are keyed into your system by hand. Purchase Orders should not be necessary, a simple letter of agreement should cover the arrangements for each item. However, if you find it necessary to use Purchase Orders, the Purchase Orders can be created with the signal to fill a requirement or as the requirement is being filled, at the same time the Accounts Receivable for the vendor and Accounts Payable for your company can be set up. The PO can be opened and closed simultaneously when the requirement is filled. This also works well for consignment inventory. However, in this case of consignment inventory, you are clearly responsible for maintaining your vendor's inventory and are responsible for its care as soon as the inventory comes into your possession.

Remember the inventory in the in-house store is the property of your vendor. Don't be surprised when he removes material from your in-house store for another one of his Customers. This arrangement can be attractive for the vendor. He may view your stocking location as a place to store material for his other nearby Customers. He may even drum up new business in your area by touting the stocking location. Provided this does not get out of hand, you should not discourage this behavior. It will only serve to further cement your relationship by making your in-house store arrangement more attractive and more valuable to the vendor.

The In-house Store

What is in it For Your Supplier?

The supplier has much to gain from an in-house store arrangement:

- He gains a Customer who commits to purchase an entire category of merchandise for a specified period of time, usually a year at a given price.
- The chances of the relationship continuing, once the in-house store has been established, are excellent.
- The vendor learns how to service his Customers in this manner.
- He can use the success of your operation to demonstrate to prospective Customers what he can bring to their party.
- Having a representative in your organization, the Store Keeper, who will easily learn what is going on in your operation, will help your vendor in his search for new opportunities to sell you other items.
- You will be constantly looking for ways to expand the lines your vendor carries in the in-house store. This will give the vendor an easy outlet for new items added to his line, making it less risky to add new items. Also, you will be migrating away from your other suppliers in favor of placing items in the in-house store to lower your inventory.
- He gets a place to store inventory for his other Customers in the area.

What is in it for You?

You should be highly motivated to encourage your vendors to provide you with in-house store services:

- You gain the material flexibility you need to drastically reduce your inventory and improve your throughput velocity. Even though the inventory is at your disposal at a

moment's notice, it is on your vendor's books, not yours, until you draw it out of the store.
- A key part of the flexibility you gain will enable you to react to changes in your Customer's requirements. When the material is immediately available, you just add labor and equipment and you have product to satisfy your Customer's requirements.
- You have an assured supply of material at an agreed upon price for a long period.
- The opportunities to simplify your backroom operations are tremendous. You do not have to receive the material, stock the material, find the material or distribute the material. The return material process is simplified – just take it back to the store. Purchase Orders, Purchase Order maintenance, matching invoices, etc., are eliminated. All this will greatly simplify your operation. You may not start out taking advantage of all these opportunities at first, but they are there and you can gravitate toward their benefit.
- The elimination of material transactions on your Shop Floor was mentioned above. Preventing these errors will save many thousands of dollars and much grief. One of the most common causes of part shortages is an incorrectly keyed transaction. With this process you have the opportunity to virtually eliminate keyed transactions.
- You save the labor in the services provided by the Store Keeper, who is an employee of your vendor.
- Communication with your vendor is regularly ongoing. Issues like quality problems are communicated quickly through the in-house Store Keeper.

For an exercise, add up the value of all the items you currently have in your own stockrooms that could reasonably be placed in one or two in-house stores. This is the inventory reduction you

The In-house Store

are looking at when you start your in-house store. You probably will be able to convince your in-house store vendors to add items to their line for you, increasing the inventory savings as you go. Also, as you design new products with new parts, these items will be added to the store. With our last electronics store, a few of the items we were able to convince the vendor to add were small tools, assembled circuit boards, and completed 14 and 17 inch monitors.

One of my most successful in-house stores that included a Store Keeper provided by my vendor was in a factory whose direct labor force was represented by the Teamsters Union. If you cultivate good Union relations with your local, they will cooperate on issues like this. I have operated with several different Unions for over 22 years of my career and I can truly say that they have cooperated with virtually all the Lean-flow Manufacturing endeavors undertaken in these Union shops.

The in-house store concept works well for many different commodities. They work especially well for electronic components. However, I have seen them used for everything from sheet metal parts to product operating manuals. I have never seen an in-house store that was a failure, at least not for the Customer.

Summary:

The in-house store concept provides your company access to a defined inventory of parts that are owned by your vendor and stored in your facility in a secured area that you provide your vendor. Material ownership transfers to you at the time the Store Keeper of the in-house store delivers the parts to a designated area in your facility. The Stock Keeper is on your vendor's payroll, not yours. The Stock Keeper can be a full time position or a part time position, depending on how much business is involved.

The in-house store can be a good deal for your supplier and a good deal for you. The supplier gains a steady high volume

Customer with a high probability of increased future business. Your business gains material flexibility that will help you dramatically reduce your inventory and increase your throughput velocity. You also gain opportunities for backroom transaction simplification through the close-working relationship you develop with your supplier. And don't forget the services provided by the vendor's Stock Keeper, which you normally would have to perform with your own employees.

CHAPTER 7

The "Bread Man Routine"

In this chapter we will discuss in detail the concept of the "Bread Man routine," the second of the three primary methods of bringing material into your facility. With this concept, you contract with a supplier to not only deliver material to your Shop Floor, but also to replenish that material in the designated areas of your factory as the material is consumed. The vendor is charged with the responsibility of insuring that you never run out of the material he provides in the appointed areas where the material is consumed. This method is called the "Bread Man routine" because of the concept's similarity to the method commonly used in supermarkets to replenish the bread supply. The bread company takes on the responsibility of stocking the supermarket shelves, ensuring a never-ending supply of fresh bread. The bread company analyzes the supermarket's usage and adjusts deliveries accordingly. Very often, the bread company is aware of the changes in demand for its products even before the supermarket's Management realizes the changes have taken place.

The program can be as flexible as one's imagination. A given vendor can be responsible for filling a specified color bin, no matter where the bin is located in the facility. In one of my most recent factories one supplier was responsible for filling all the blue bins with hardware. Each bin was labeled with the part number of the part the bin held and the minimum number of parts that were supposed to be present.

This system can be very visual. The supplier just keeps the blue or red or green bins filled on a daily basis. The bins can also be marked with a fill level. This can be as simple as a line on the bin indicating the level at which the bin is to be filled. When the fill level is visible, the supplier fills the bin with the appropriate part. Assigning different color bins to different suppliers allows you to assess the level of service you are getting from a supplier simply by walking around and viewing the levels in the color bins that supplier is responsible for. Should a shortage occur, everyone will immediately know which supplier to go after for resolution. Different color bins can also be used to distinguish between categories of parts. For instance: all stainless steel hardware is stored in orange bins and all cadmium-plated hardware is stored in yellow bins. One can also use different color bins to distinguish which material is used on which product. Material stored in blue bins is used to build product "X" and material stored in green bins is used to build product "Y."

One important distinguishing factor that sets this method of material replenishment apart from either the in-house store or the Wand-to-order methods of material replenishment is that your employees have nothing to do with signaling the need to deliver material. This is completely the responsibility of the supplier who has been selected to supply the material.

Should the supplier have difficulty delivering an item, the supplier must be proactive about informing you, his Customer, as early as possible. These occurrences had better be very rare. When this does occur, the supplier should take the necessary action to procure the same material or if necessary, an approved substitute, until his regular supply is restored. Any additional cost associated with supplying an approved alternate, such as a superior part, should be borne by the supplier. These issues should be covered by the formal agreement with your vendor.

The "Bread Man Routine"

The Agreement

The agreement should cover:

- The part numbers the vendor will be responsible for delivering.
- The price you will pay for each part.
- The "letter of intent," if there is one.
- How often you will quote the operation to the competition – usually no more often than once a year.
- How the quote will be constructed. Usually you will insist that the vendor sell you the material covered by the agreement at a price equal to or lower than you can buy it for elsewhere. Again, as with your in-house store, you must be reasonable here. By reasonable I mean allowing comparisons based on a basket of parts. Your vendor may lose because he is a penny higher on a fastener; however, he may be 4 pennies cheaper on two other fasteners. Switching away from a reliable supplier is not only risky, but a lot of work, as well as costly. Don't change "Bread Man" vendors for a few cents on a part.
- Actions the vendor is expected to take when his normal supply of material is interrupted.
    - Who bears the extra cost to buy the parts elsewhere or the design costs to redesign another replacement part into your product?
    - Process for obtaining permission to substitute material.
    - Proper notification procedures for substituted material.
- Separation agreement.
- Designated areas to be supplied.
- Access to your facility.
- Frequency of coverage.

- How much material the vendor is expected to be able to supply, i.e., 150% over your normal usage as reflected in your Material Requirements Planning monthly requirements report.
- How you will communicate future requirements to your supplier.

Transaction Simplification

As with the in-house store, there are many opportunities to simplify the business transactions between you and your supplier. This can be done electronically, setting up the Accounts Receivable for the vendor and Accounts Payable for you when material is transacted onto your Shop Floor. In this situation you will probably want your supplier to initiate the transactions even if they are done on your Shop Floor. The material involved in the "Bread Man routine" is usually very inexpensive and is often expensed on receipt, making inventory transactions unnecessary. If you have a need to check your vendor's honesty and integrity, you can always compare your billings for any given part against your requirements or past usage. Hopefully you will trust the vendors you choose to enter into these types of close relationships with.

If you do not expense the material, the receiving transaction can move the material into your inventory. The material is then transacted out of your inventory when the finished goods item is transacted to final stock through the "backflushing" method based on your bills-of-materials. With this system all your material movement transactions are done electronically, eliminating the hundreds of errors normally created when thousands of items are keyed into your system by hand. Purchase Orders should not be necessary; a simple letter of agreement should cover the arrangements for each item. However, if you find it necessary to use Purchase Orders, the Purchase Orders can be created with the receiving signal when material is received in your facility. At the time of material receipt, your Accounts Payable can be set up and your vendor's Accounts Receivable can be created. The Purchase Order can be opened and closed simultaneously because the requirement is filled when the material is received.

What is in it for Your Supplier?

The supplier has much to gain from a "Bread Man routine" relationship:

- He gains a Customer who commits to purchase an entire category of merchandise for a specified period of time, usually a year at a given price.
- The chances of the relationship continuing, once the Supplier has been selected, are excellent.
- The vendor learns how to service his Customers in this manner.
- He can use the success of your operation to demonstrate to prospective Customers what he can bring to their party.
- Having a representative in your organization, the bin filler, on a regular basis will make it easy for the vendor to learn what is going on in your operation, helping him in his search for new opportunities to sell you other items.
- You will be constantly looking for ways to expand the lines your vendor supplies through the "Bread Man routine." This will give the vendor an easy outlet for new items added to his line, making it less risky to add new items. Also, you will be migrating away from your other suppliers in favor of adding items to the "Bread Man routine" to lower your inventory.
- He increases the overall volume of the material he contracts for.

What is in it For You?

You should be highly motivated to encourage your vendors to serve you through the "Bread Man routine:"

- You gain the material flexibility you need to drastically reduce your inventory and improve your throughput velocity. Even though the inventory is at your disposal at a moment's notice, it is on your vendor's books until he fills your bins, and then you can negotiate a deal whereby you pay for the material 30 or 60 days after the bins are filled.

- A key part of the flexibility you gain will enable you to react to changes in your Customer's requirements. When the material is immediately available, you just add labor and equipment and you have product to satisfy your Customer's requirements.

- You have an assured supply of material at an agreed upon price for a long period.

- The opportunities to simplify your backroom operations are tremendous. You do not have to receive the material, stock the material, find the material or distribute the material. The return material process is simplified – just have the vendor take it back on the next fill day. Purchase Orders, Purchase Order maintenance, matching invoices, etc., are eliminated. All this will greatly simplify your operation. You may not start out taking advantage of all these opportunities at first, but they are there and you can gravitate toward their benefit.

- The elimination of material transactions on your Shop Floor was mentioned above. Preventing these errors will save many dollars and much grief. One of the most common causes of part shortages is an incorrectly keyed transaction. With this process you have the opportunity to virtually eliminate keyed transactions.

The "Bread Man Routine"

- You save the labor in the service provided by the supplying vendor who is filling your bins.
- Communication with your vendor is regularly ongoing. Issues like quality problems are communicated quickly through daily contact with your employees.

You can repeat the inventory reduction analysis exercise given in the last chapter by adding up the value of all the items you currently have in your own stockrooms that could reasonably be covered under the "Bread Man routine" described here. This is the inventory reduction you are looking at to start. You probably will be able to convince your suppliers to add items to their line for you, increasing the inventory savings as you go. Also, as you design new products with new parts, these items can be added to the "Bread Man routine."

And I will mention again that my last facility's labor force was represented by the Teamsters Union. If you cultivate good Union relations with your local, they will cooperate on issues like this. Progressive Unions have come to realize that their success is closely tied to the success of the companies whose labor they represent.

The "Bread Man routine" concept works well for many different commodities. It works especially well for hardware, wire, supplies and low cost electronic components. However, as I have mentioned earlier in this book, a German company I was responsible for converting to flow manufacturing successfully used the "Bread Man routine" for machined parts. Their hardware vendor was so pleased with the direction the relationship between the two companies was taking, that he expanded his business by bidding on all the machined parts used in the facility. The "Bread Man routine" vendor won most of the bids and eventually supplied the bulk of the machined parts used in the facility in addition to the hardware.

Summary

The "Bread Man routine" concept for acquiring material provides your company access to a defined inventory of parts that your vendor will deliver directly to your Shop Floor or workbench when the vendor determines there is a need, using a prescribed criteria. The material is owned by your vendor until under the criteria a need for a material delivery occurs. Material ownership transfers to you at the time the material is placed in the designated bins. The bin filler is on your vendor's payroll, not yours.

The "Bread Man routine" can be a good deal for your supplier and a good deal for you. The supplier gains a steady high volume Customer with a high probability of increased future business. Your business gains material flexibility that will help you dramatically reduce your inventory and increase your throughput velocity. You also gain opportunities for backroom transaction simplification through the close working relationship you develop with your supplier. You also save on the inventory control services and the bin filling services provided by your vendor that would normally have to be performed by your own employees.

CHAPTER 8

Wand-to-order

In this chapter we will discuss in detail the vendor Kanban concept of Wand-to-order. The first of this simple three piece methodology for bringing material into your facility from someone else's stockroom rather than your own was the in-house store covered in Chapter 6; the second, covered in Chapter 7, was the "Bread Man routine;" the third, Wand-to-order, we are about to cover here. Together these three methods of delivering material to the factory will revolutionize the way you do business. They will create an amazing amount of flexibility, allowing for dramatic improvements in inventory turns and cycle time.

The Wand-to-order method works by scanning a bar code with a wand scanner, if you have an automated Shop Floor information system, to send a Kanban signal to your vendor, requesting delivery of a pre-arranged quantity of material. Your vendor has a very short window of time to deliver the material called for by the Kanban signal, usually within one to two days. This can be a very efficient method of ordering material. It places the initiating action for the ordering responsibility with the Shop Floor worker. When the minimum is reached, the Shop Floor operator requiring the material scans a Kanban card from the materials point of use location on the Shop Floor. The signal can be sent directly to the vendor by e-mail, fax or direct link to your operating system. An automated system is not absolutely necessary to use this delivery system. In the absence of an automated data collection system and scanning abilities, the Kanban cards can be collected and faxed or phoned to the supplier.

One caution here: If your employees are like me, and they have been burned by running out of the same part over and over, they may just take that wand and wand that card ten times to be sure they never run out of that part again. We all know this is not the way to fix a delivery problem, don't we? However, sometimes emotions get involved and we need to guard against this possibility. A fail-safe can be added to the system that reroutes every Kanban part that is scanned more than twice in the same day to a buyer for review, before sending the signal on to the supplier.

Usually, look-up tables are designed so that when a Kanban part number is scanned, the system references the look-up table to determine: the quantity to be ordered, the vendor to order the part from (send the signal to), and the agreed upon price to be paid. With this information the order can be sent directly – by e-mail (intranet or internet) or sent with a fax server to your supplier. To carry this one step further and streamline your backroom operation, you can set up the Accounts Payable according to terms you agreed to in the supplier "letter of intent." Your vendor can also streamline his operation by allowing the signal, when received and fulfilled on his end, to set up his Accounts Receivable. Using these systems in this fashion can eliminate tons of unnecessary paperwork in both your operation and in your vendor's operation. The name of the game is the elimination of unnecessary work or waste.

This method works well with local certified suppliers who can deliver directly to your Shop Floor. The system, referring to the instructions stored in the look-up table, can direct the vendor to the correct location inside your facility to deliver the material. Of course, the vendors who are allowed to deliver directly to your

Shop Floor must be certified. Their acceptable quality levels must meet your requirements as proven by their historical track record for delivering a quality product.

A reliable certified vendor program is necessary for all of the three methods of delivering material directly to your factory floor. Each vendor will be certified as a vendor that is capable of complying consistently with your quality requirements. After the supplier is qualified, each component that supplier provides directly to your Shop Floor should be certified. You will find that not all suppliers can meet your standards for every different item they supply. If a supplier provides 50 different items and 49 out of 50 meet your requirements, you will be able to certify only 49 of the 50 parts to be delivered directly to your Shop Floor. The 50th part will have to endure a visit to your Inspection Department until the part can be certified for delivery directly to your Shop Floor. I will cover certified vendor programs in more detail in another chapter on the subject later in this book.

As with the other two methods of delivering material to your Shop Floor, should the supplier have difficulty delivering an item, the supplier must be proactive about informing you as early as possible. Again, these occurrences had better be very rare or you should be looking for a replacement supplier. When this does occur, the supplier should take the necessary action to procure the same material or if necessary, an approved substitute for the material until his regular supply is restored. Any additional cost associated with supplying an approved alternate, such as a superior part, should be borne by the supplier. Again, these issues should be covered by the formal agreement with your vendor.

The Agreement

The agreement should cover:

- The part numbers the vendor will be responsible for supplying.

- The price you will pay for each part.
- The "letter of intent," if there is one.
- How often you will quote the parts involved to the competition – here again, usually no more than once a year.
- How the quote will be constructed. Usually you will insist that the vendor sell you the material at a price equal to or lower than you can buy it for elsewhere. Again, as with your in-house store and the "Bread Man routine," you must be reasonable here. By reasonable I mean allowing comparisons based on a basket of parts. Remember, switching away from a reliable supplier is risky, costly and a lot of work. Don't change vendors to save a few dollars.
- Actions the vendor is expected to take when his normal supply of material is interrupted.
  - Who bears the extra cost to buy the parts elsewhere or the design costs to redesign another replacement part into your product?
  - Process for obtaining permission to substitute material.
  - Proper notification procedures for substituted material.
- Separation agreement
- Designated areas in your facility to be supplied.
- Access to your facility.
- How much material the vendor is expected to be able to supply, i.e., 150% over your normal usage as reflected in your Material Requirements Planning monthly requirements report.
- How you will communicate future requirements to your supplier.

Wand-to-order

Transaction Simplification

As with the in-house store and "Bread Man routine," there are opportunities to simplify the business transactions between you and your supplier. As mentioned above, this can be done electronically, setting up the Accounts Receivable for the vendor and Accounts Payable for you when your vendor acknowledges the Kanban signal and material is sent, or when the material is transacted onto your Shop Floor (received). The transaction can also transfer the material into your inventory automatically at the same time. The material can then be transacted out of your inventory when the finished good item is transacted to final stock through the "backflushing" method based on your bills-of-materials. Again, with this system virtually all your material movement transactions are done electronically, eliminating the hundreds of errors normally created when thousands of items are keyed into your system by hand. Here, too, Purchase Orders should not be necessary; a simple letter of agreement should cover the arrangements for each item. Look for the chapter on letters of agreement later in this book. However, if you find it necessary to use Purchase Orders, the Purchase Orders can be created with the signal to fill a requirement or as the requirement is being filled, at the same time the Accounts Receivable for the vendor and Accounts Payable for your company can be set up. The Purchase Order can be opened and closed simultaneously when the requirement is filled.

What is in it For Your Supplier?

As with the other two methods of procuring material, the in-house store and the "Bread Man routine," the supplier has much to gain from a Wand-to-order arrangement:

- He gains a Customer who commits to purchase an entire category of merchandise for a specified period of time, usually a year at a given price.

- The chances of the relationship continuing, once the arrangement is entered into, is excellent.
- The vendor learns how to service his Customers in this manner.
- He can use the success of your operation to demonstrate to prospective Customers what he can bring to their party.
- You will be constantly looking for ways to expand the part numbers covered by the arrangement. This will give the vendor an easy outlet for new items added to his line, making it less risky on his part to add new items. Also, you will be migrating away from your other suppliers in favor of placing items with the vendor using the "Wand-to-order method."
- You will do everything you can to assist the vendor in improving his ability to react quickly to your demands, while keeping his inventory at a minimum. Remember the example earlier in the book where we were able to help our vendor improve his operation by redesigning some of our parts and recommending the addition of certain types of equipment. This kind of close working relationship strengthens both organizations and seals lasting relationships.

What is in it For You?

As with the in-house store and the "Bread Man routine," you should be highly motivated to encourage your vendors to provide you with these types of services:

- You gain the material flexibility you need to drastically reduce your inventory and improve your throughput velocity. All the material not covered by the in-house store or the "Bread Man routine" can be supplied by this method, rounding out your flexibility options for delivery of material. The inventory is available to you on short notice. It is

Wand-to-order

on your vendor's books, not yours, until he delivers based on your Kanban signal for the material delivery.

- A key part of the flexibility you gain will enable you to react to changes in your Customer's requirements. When the material is available on short notice, you just add labor and equipment and you have product to satisfy your Customer's requirements.

- You have an assured supply of material at an agreed upon price for a long period of time.

- As with the other two methods of acquiring material, the opportunities to simplify your backroom operations are tremendous. You do not have to stock the material, find the material or distribute the material. Purchase Orders, Purchase Order maintenance, matching invoices, etc., are eliminated. All this will greatly simplify your operation. You may not start out taking advantage of all these opportunities at first, but they are there and you can gravitate toward their benefit.

- The elimination of material transactions on your Shop Floor was mentioned above. Preventing these errors will save many thousands of dollars and much grief. Again, one of the most common causes of part shortages are incorrectly keyed transactions. With this process you have the opportunity to virtually eliminate keyed transactions.

- Communication with your vendor is regularly ongoing. Issues like quality problems are communicated quickly.

You can continue to calculate your potential inventory savings by adding up the value of all the items you currently have in your own stockrooms that could reasonably be placed in a Wand-to-order type program. You probably will be able to add new items to the Wand-to-order agreement as time goes on, increasing the inventory savings as you go.

I have used all three of these delivery techniques successfully in more than one factory. They are fun to implement and yield huge inventory savings quickly. By increasing flexibility through the continuous availability of material on short notice, you will be able to delight your Customers by responding to their ever-changing requirements. All this and, at the same time, lowering your overall costs. What could be better to insure the future health of your business?

The Wand-to-order concept works well for many different commodities. It works especially well for sheet metal, machined parts, weldments, manuals and bulky shipping containers. However, just about any commodity can be brought into your facility in this fashion. Again, use this method for any item that does not fit the in-house store or the "Bread Man routine."

Summary

The Wand-to-order method works by scanning a bar code with a scanner, if you have an automated Shop Floor information system, to send a Kanban signal to your vendor, requesting delivery of a pre-arranged quantity of material. Your vendor has a very short window of time to deliver the material called for by the Kanban signal, usually within one to two days. It places the initiating action for the ordering responsibility with the Shop Floor worker. When the minimum is reached, the Shop Floor operator requiring the material scans a Kanban card from the materials point of use location on the Shop Floor. The signal can be sent directly to the vendor by e-mail, fax or direct link to your operating system. In the absence of an automated data collection system and scanning abilities, the Kanban cards can be collected and faxed or phoned to the supplier.

As with the other two methods of acquiring material, the in-house store and the "Bread Man routine," the Wand-to-order method of acquiring material can be a good deal for your supplier and a good deal for you. The supplier gains a steady high volume

Wand-to-order

Customer with a high probability of increased future business. Your business gains material flexibility that will help you dramatically reduce your inventory and increase your throughput velocity. You also gain opportunities for backroom transaction simplification through the close working relationships you develop with your suppliers.

CHAPTER 9

Letters of Intent

The "letter of intent" is a simple agreement between you and your supplier that describes your intention to purchase a specific item or items over a given period of time. The "letter of intent" can replace a Purchase Order or other type of contract in the vast majority of procurement situations. It should only be used with a trusted supplier partner. It is necessary for a level of trust to exist between you and your supplier for this loose form of agreement to work. The real intended purpose of an agreement to purchase material between vendor and purchaser is to remind both parties of their obligations under the agreement. The thousands of agreements entered into annually by the average business are not entered into with the intention of needing enforcement of any kind through arbitration, the court system, etc. A very very small number of these contracts ever reach the stage where either party is forced to take enforcement action against the other. And none of them should have been entered into with the intention of having to take an action to force the other party to comply with the covenants of the agreement. Of course there are exceptions to some of these common sense statements. When dealing with certain types of purchases, there are specific types of contracts required by law, such as transferring Real Property, some forms of Government contracting, etc. But for the vast majority of day-to-day purchases between supplier and manufacturer, the form of the agreement is moot from a legal perspective. Under these circumstances use the simplest form of agreement possible that will serve your purposes. If you are in any way unsure about your particular situation, by all means check with your legal folks and ask their assistance in working out a simplified form of agreement that you can use in your dealings. None of this is presented or intended as legal advice, but rather as ideas to stimulate your thinking in the direction of simplifying your business dealings with your suppliers.

The Letter

The "letter of intent" should cover the following:

- Items to be purchased – a description of the item, usually the part number will suffice.

- The quantity of material to be covered by the "letter of intent" – the quantity can be vague or specific. Usually the quantity is expressed in terms of a forecast. The next 6 to 12 months forecast will be called out in the letter, along with a provision for communicating changes to the forecast. In the absence of a forecast the quantity can be expressed in terms of a range. Company A intends to purchase between 50 and 100 of part "X" over the next 12 months.

- Pricing – The price to be paid for each item and their volume discount levels. Under what circumstances will the vendor be allowed to increase the price; i.e., a price increase of two percent may kick in 30 days after the price of copper increases by more than 10%.

- The beginning and ending period covered by the agreement.

- The method of signaling – how you will signal the vendor to deliver material. e-mail, fax, phone or mail, etc.

- Delivery requirements – The number of days or hours that the supplier has to deliver the material after receiving the signal to deliver.
- Shipping point – i.e., FOB Shipping point.
- Ship via – i.e., Delivery or Truck or Air, etc.
- Freight Terms – i.e., Prepay or Prepay and add to the invoice or freight collect.
- Payment terms and discount – i.e., one percent discount – 10 days, net 60 days.
- Packaging requirements – i.e., each item is to be delivered on a skid or 10 items packaged in a clear Poly bag that is to be clearly labeled with a part number and bar code representing the part number and quantity.
- Who pays additional costs when substitutions are required? Should the supplier have to substitute an approved, more expensive component for the specified component, who will be responsible for paying the additional cost?
- Supplier quality – Minimum quality standards, process controls, quality reports and reviews should be mentioned. Remedies and consequences for poor quality should be spelled out. Under what circumstances does a certified part lose its certification and a certified vendor loses his or her certification? Who pays for the repair when it is necessary to repair material received from the vendor, etc.
- How often the entire package under agreement will be re-quoted – usually no more often than once a year. It will be too costly and time consuming to change suppliers more often than once a year, and it is unlikely that you will

be able to interest a supplier for a period of less than one year.

- Right to review, change or cancel the agreement – under what circumstances can the agreement be cancelled or amended. Delivery problems, quality problems or non-competitive pricing are some of the usual reasons for amendment or cancellation.
- Separation and cancellation provisions – this should specify the amount of material you will be responsible for, if and when you terminate the agreement. This can be stated simply, such as, company "A" will be responsible to take delivery of no more than a two months supply of those items that are custom built for company "A." Calculation of a two months supply will be determined by using the average monthly delivery of the material delivered over the last six months. Also, the length of notice required for separation should be spelled out.
- You can add any boilerplate that is necessary for your particular business.

Following are some points to consider when paying cancellation charges on those occasions when it is necessary to cancel a purchase agreement for material. Provided the supplier is one with which you have had and/or expect to continue to have a business relationship with, you will have considerable clout and you should use it wisely.

- Never allow a supplier in these circumstances to make a profit on your misfortune.
- If the material was designed and built to your specifications, offer to reimburse the supplier for the material, labor and other costs incurred, but stop short of paying him or her for the profit portion of the cancelled item.

Letters of Intent

- If the item can be sold to another user easily, you should pay no cancellation charges except for any small costs, such as freight charges, incurred by your supplier.
- Given an ongoing relationship between you and your supplier, this approach is only fair.

Caution must be exercised when dealing with price increases. Remember, the only good deal is a deal that is good for both parties. The intent is to partner with your supplier, not to profit at his expense. It is suggested that the agreement state that the price is to be held firm and then list any exceptions such as: changes in market conditions or the presence of competitive pricing that differs markedly from the agreement price. This leaves the door open for price increases or price decreases. The agreement can call for the supplier to disclose his costs in order to justify any price increase or decrease. Also, both partners should only accept price increases or decreases by mutual consent after the agreement is signed. In most cases, you clearly have the upper hand here, because you have the checkbook. Don't abuse it. The vendor can charge you anything he wants; however, you are only going to pay what you perceive is the agreed upon price. An in-house store agreement may simply state that the vendor must supply all the components in the store at the same or a better price than you can buy them for anywhere else. Again, be reasonable, allow your vendor to bundle groups of components for purposes of comparison. He may be more expensive on one component, but make up for it on another.

It is wise to enter into an agreement with your supplier that calls for sharing any cost savings that are achieved through joint effort. Earlier in this book an excellent example of this type of activity was given when a Manufacturing Engineer from one of my companies devoted one or two days a week to assisting a vendor in reducing inventory and improving cycle time. Your supplier will often come up with cost saving ideas that require your help to implement. For instance: a change may require that you perform testing to validate the effect of the change. Even though your vendor came up with the idea, you did the work of implementing the change on your end and you should share in the benefit. In addition to testing, you will have to change drawings and specifications. A regular ongoing cost-reduction program should be in place in your organization with devoted resources whose focus is reducing product costs. Too many companies believe that the product engineering effort is over once the product is out of the design stage. Sustaining engineering can be a tremendously profitable endeavor. It is important to define where in your organization this responsibility lies. The responsibility for sustaining engineering can remain with the Engineering group or be handled by the Manufacturing Engineering group. Unfortunately, too many companies fail to define who in their organization is responsible for this effort or they fail to set formal goals to be achieved; consequently no one owns or harvests this lucrative opportunity.

And finally you may want to add a statement that the agreement is not meant to be legally binding on either party.

By all means, consult your legal experts prior to using a "letter of intent" to purchase. However, the burdens of making your legal folks understand what is at stake here rests with the operations folks. Make your legal group understand the importance of letters of intent and they will support your efforts here.

Summary

The "letter of intent" is a simple agreement between you and your supplier that describes your intention to purchase a specific item or items over a given period of time. It is necessary for a level of trust to exist between you and your supplier for this loose form of agreement to work. The real intended purpose of the agreement is to remind both parties of their obligations under the agreement. A very few of these contracts ever reach the stage

Letters of Intent

where either party is forced to take enforcement action against the other. And none of them should have been entered into with the intention of having to take an action to force the other party to comply with the covenants of the agreement. For the vast majority of day-to-day purchases between supplier and manufacturer, the form of the agreement is moot from a legal perspective. Under these circumstances use the simplest form of agreement possible that will serve your purposes. If you are in any way unsure about your particular situation, by all means check with your legal folks and ask their assistance in working out a simplified form of agreement that you can use in your dealings. None of this is presented or intended as legal advice, but rather as ideas to stimulate your thinking in the direction of simplifying your business dealings with your suppliers.

Other considerations can include:

- Paying cancellation charges — Never allow partnering suppliers in these circumstances to make a profit on your misfortune. If the material was designed and built to your specifications, offer to reimburse the supplier for the material, labor and other costs incurred, but stop short of paying him or her for the profit portion of the cancelled item.
- Price increases — Remember, the only good deal is a deal that is good for both parties. The intent is to partner with your supplier, not to profit at his expense. It is suggested that the agreement state that the price is to be held firm and then list any exceptions.
- Sharing cost savings — It is wise to enter into an agreement with your supplier that calls for sharing any cost savings that are achieved through joint effort. Even though your vendor came up with the idea, you did the work of implementing the change on your end and you should share in the benefit.

- Sustaining engineering – Failure to formally define where this responsibility lies will result in no one harvesting this lucrative opportunity.

CHAPTER 10

Point of Use

In this chapter we continue laying out the plans for your new Millennium factory with a discussion about point of use material storage, delivery and usage. This is a key element in the Lean-flow of material into and through your linked-cell factory. If you are going to run a factory with a fraction of the material you use to have present in your push manufacturing facility, that material must be on station and ready to contribute to the manufacturing process. There will be no time to receive material, inspect material, queue the material for stock, stock the material, kit the material, queue for material shortage cleanup and queue the material for the build process to begin. There will also be no time for all the thousands of transactions necessary to track all these functions, not to mention all the time it takes to correct all the errors caused by all these transactions.

Point of use stocking is just that, stocking the material in the manufacturing cell where it is used in the product build process. The material is received and delivered directly to the manufacturing cell or cells in the factory where the material is consumed. The only time an item is stocked in the warehouse or stockroom is when the material is so bulky that it would be detrimental to the efficient operation of the manufacturing cell.

Neatness First and Foremost

NEVER over stock the manufacturing cell with material to the point it detracts from optimum efficiency in the process of building your product. This includes, and this is especially important, the environmental aesthetics of the cell. It is very important that each cell not only be efficient but also appear neat and orderly. Your employees cannot be expected to perform operations in a neat, orderly and efficient manner, if the area they are asked to perform in is cluttered and disorderly. A cluttered and disorderly area will have a profoundly negative effect on the way your employees perform their work and handle your product.

I was asked to review the progress of a factory in the Midwest a few years ago that was attempting to implement a Lean-flow Manufacturing system. I looked over the pilot-manufacturing cell, which was overrun with material. In an attempt to stock the related material at the point of use, the stockroom containing all of the material required to build the pilot product was emptied into the manufacturing cell. When I asked the Shop Floor workers assigned to the cell how they liked the new cell layout, they did not hesitate to complain about the claustrophobic feeling inside the manufacturing cell. Material was piled so high that the walls could not be seen from anyplace in the manufacturing cell. Later that day I was asked by the Vice President of Operations for the facility and his Plant Manager what I thought of their progress. When I related that the employees were not happy about the high volume of material stocked in the cell, I was told that they had heard the same complaints before, which were to be ignored as just so much grousing. I told them that the problem was real and that even if it were not real, to the employees assigned to that cell it was a perceived problem. A perceived problem must be dealt with, especially on a pilot project. To fail in the pilot stage places the entire project in jeopardy. It is now almost three years later and the progress in that factory's efforts toward Lean

Manufacturing is pathetic, despite help from some of the leading consultants in the field. They don't get it. They think they can do these things without the support of their front line employees. Never happen! Listen closely to your people or fail!!

My rule in any factory that I have been responsible for is: You must be able to see all four walls in the factory, when you stand in any linked-manufacturing cell. If you can't see all four walls, you need to get to work on cleaning the clutter out of your factory. Schedule regular cleanup days. All employees should be expected to contribute. Get all that cardboard off the Shop Floor. Roll large trash barrels into the work areas to be filled. Remove and retire old equipment that is no longer used. This will also reduce the number of pieces of equipment needing calibration at regular intervals. It could also reduce your depreciation expense. Top Management should support, encourage and recognize the cleanup effort.

Deliver Material Directly to the Production Cell

Whenever possible, material should be delivered directly to the work cell. This happens as a matter of course with the "Bread Man routine" method of inventory replenishment. With the in-house store method of material replenishment, material is only being drawn as needed from the in-house store. This can be in hourly or daily increments. With the Wand-to-order method, the workers in the linked-cells are ordering the material. Provided the parts requested are certified and the supplying vendor is certified, the material can be delivered directly to the requesting cell. Other provisions will have to be made for material that requires in-house inspection. It is important that the material needing inspection not find its way to the work cell prior to passing inspection. It is equally important that this material be delivered to the consuming work cell immediately after passing inspection. Remember, we have no provision for queue time in the inspection area. This will have to be built into your Kanban quantity. This extra material in Kanban quantity to allow for inspection time is waste and must be eliminated as soon as possible. The way to eliminate the waste is to eliminate the need for the inspection by certifying a vendor to deliver directly to the Shop Floor. There should be very few parts needing inspection on delivery. You can see why your certification program is so important to the overall success of your Lean-Manufacturing effort and inventory reduction program. Every time you certify a part you can reduce the Kanban size by the extra material required to cover the inspection time. For an exercise that will reveal what kind of inventory reduction this effort can deliver, take all the parts you currently inspect, calculate the queue time for each part and multiply that by the average daily usage for the part. Multiply the number of parts times the part cost, add them up and there is your low hanging fruit. Transfer this money from your Inspection Department to your bank account by eliminating the inspection and then don't forget to celebrate.

Some parts will be used in more than one cell. You will have several options to choose from in handling this situation. One method that I have successfully used was to store the component in the cell that had the highest usage for the component. In this case, operators in a different cell from the stocking cell would be responsible for retrieving parts from the cell with the highest usage. Another alternative is to store the component in each cell that the component is used in. Still a third method is to do a combination of both. This is not as big a problem as it seems at first glance. First, your "Bread Man routine" deals with this problem by causing your vendor to either refill the bins in each cell using it or to fill the bin for the component in a central location that is accessible to all your employees. Most likely the components that are used in multiple cells are items like nuts, bolts and screws, and these items are usually covered by the "Bread Man routine" anyway. The items in your in-house stores are also accessible to all from one central stocking location. That leaves items that are

Point of Use

procured through the Wand-to-order method. These items are the least likely to be used in more than one cell. They are usually weldments, sheet metal parts, etc. These types of components are usually peculiar to a product or group of products that would be made in the same cell, if your cells were set up properly, that is. For sure there will be exceptions; however, they should be few enough that it is not a big deal to manage them. If you run into issues in this area, take a look at further combining more like products. Trouble with the same parts being used in multiple cells (other than hardware) usually indicates that enough combining of like products has not taken place.

Keep Your Kanban Quantities Small

It is important to keep your Kanban quantities small. First, this is a most important contributor to your inventory reduction program. The fewer assets we employ and the shorter time we have them in our possession before converting them to finished goods that are transferable to our Customers' inventory and hence our Accounts Receivable, the more efficient we will become at using our inventory assets. Second, small Kanban quantities enable us to store material at the point of use without cluttering up our manufacturing cells. Another benefit, that we will discuss further in a later chapter, is the cost of quality and how it can be improved by reducing the cost of scrap. If you have fewer components in your inventory when you discover a defect, you have fewer parts and/or assemblies to rework. We also have fewer parts to count in the cycle counting process and fewer parts to lose.

Warehousing

When all is said and done, you may still need a warehouse to stock the bigger bulky parts. Remember, it is much more preferable to stock parts in a warehouse than overcrowd a work cell and hinder its efficiency, real or perceived. You may have a vendor who is the only vendor on earth that can supply you with a particular part and he knows it. This vendor may well demand that you take larger deliveries than you need or want to. Also, you may want to protect your organization from scarce material shortages.

It is conceivable that you will have to take a minimum quantity and stock it in your warehouse. One of my businesses used very exotic materials and I was forced to take delivery of a several years supply on different items. One of these items was a special nickel with a carbon content that only my company's products used. This meant that I had to buy and take delivery of two ingots (the minimum) at a time. This was an eight-year supply. This also meant that I had to send the ingots, one at a time, to the rolling mills to have them rolled into so much rod, sheet and bar stock. This was a four-year supply (try forecasting these requirements). For another item, I was forced to carry a several years supply of uranium glass. This was a glass rod that contained uranium and was used to seal glass to certain metals. The glass was manufactured (melted) by only one supplier in the world, once every three years and, as you can imagine, there was not much demand for this exotic material. If you ordered the glass, you had to take delivery of the entire lot when the process was completed. In these cases it was probably wise to have control of the material so that it could be safeguarded from who knows what hazard. Also, having control of the material was a barrier to entry from any competition.

When you are forced to stock material in a separate warehouse off the Shop Floor, link the warehouse to the manufacturing cells that consume the material. You should use Kanban signals between the production cells and the warehouse. A scanner can be used to signal requirements. Scanning a Kanban card sends a signal to your business system, which refers to a look-up table and sends a signal to the warehouse detailing the part number, Kanban quantity of the material specified and the delivery point on the Shop Floor. The material is then delivered directly to the production cell. Another method of communicating requirements to the warehouse is simply collecting Kanban cards from a central collection point hourly or daily and filling these requirements from the warehouse. A little imagination goes a long way toward resolving these simple issues.

Cycle Counting

The material stocked in the production cell is considered to be material in your stockroom. Remember, in an ideal flow-manufacturing situation, for inventory classification purposes all the material in your facility engaged in the manufacturing process is classified as either raw material or finished goods – no work-in-process. (Your work-in-process material will be classified as raw material even though it may serve the traditional function of work-in-process material.) Your goal is to bring material into your factory from outside vendors in one of three ways: 1. In-house store; 2. "Bread Man routine;" 3. Wand-to-order. In each of these delivery methods you will be electronically transferring the material into your raw material inventory (the entire factory is your stockroom). When your product is completed, it will be transacted into finished goods, relieving your raw material through the backflushing process based on your bills-of-material.

Therefore, we must cycle count the inventory in our work cells based on our cycle count requirements, which are in turn based on our overall cycle count program, approved by your auditing firm. I strongly suggest that the cycle counting be done on a daily basis (only those few parts that the system chooses for that day's count—the cycle count program requires that we count only a small percentage of the total material on hand daily). If you are still taking quarterly, semi-annual or annual wall-to-wall inventories, get together with your auditing firm immediately and work out a cycle count program quickly. Your cycle count program will help ensure that your inventory counts remain accurate throughout the year. I also strongly suggest that the people doing the cycle counting be the same people assigned to the production cell. By insisting that the same people who manage the material pull systems do the cycle counting, you are reinforcing the importance of accuracy in managing the entire system. They will be forced to correct their own mistakes. No time for finger pointing at others' mistakes in these productive cells.

Summary

Point of use stocking is just that, stocking the material in the manufacturing cell where it is used in the product build process. The material is received and delivered directly to the manufacturing cell or cells in the factory where the material is consumed. If you are going to run a factory with a fraction of the material you use to have present in your push manufacturing facility, that material must be on station and ready to contribute to the manufacturing process. The only time an item is stocked in the warehouse or stockroom is when the material is so bulky that it would be detrimental to the efficient operation of the manufacturing cell. NEVER overstock the manufacturing cell with material to the point it detracts from optimum efficiency in the process of building your product.

Material should be delivered directly to the work cell. This happens as a matter of course with the "Bread Man routine" method of inventory replenishment. With the in-house store method of material replenishment, material is being drawn only as needed from the in-house store. This can be in hourly or daily increments. With the Wand-to-order method, the workers in the linked-cells are ordering the material. Provided the parts requested are certified and the supplying vendor is certified, the material can be delivered directly to the requesting cell. Other provisions will have to be made for material that requires in-house inspection. It is important to keep your Kanban

Point of Use

quantities small. Your cycle count program will help ensure that your inventory counts remain accurate within the linked-cell throughout the year.

CHAPTER 11

Certified Vendors

In this chapter we will discuss the importance of a certified vendor program and how this program will help you achieve your objective of creating an efficient new Millennium flow-manufacturing facility. Certified vendors and certified parts are crucial in achieving your objectives. Without certification your suppliers will not be able to deliver directly to your Shop Floor and material will be held in your incoming inspection area in queue, awaiting costly inspection. Your inventory goals will also be adversely impacted. If incoming material is held in queue and delayed while being inspected, you will have to have larger material Kanbans to cover this delay period, not to mention any extra inventory that you may be carrying in the event of a rejection of incoming parts. Your ability to react to changes in Customer requirements will be impaired. Any time you have a situation that adversely affects material flexibility, you will impair your ability to react quickly to your Customer's changing needs, as material sitting awaiting inspection cannot be used to satisfy your Customer requirements. Thus, velocity is negatively impacted when material flexibility is impacted.

With a good certified vendor program in place, material will move smoothly into your facility and go directly to the manufacturing cell or point of use areas consuming the material. Your certified vendors can serve you well when they are delivering certified material in one of our three chosen delivery methods: The in-house store can deliver directly to the manufacturing cell – your vendor's responsibility. Material being delivered via the "Bread Man routine" will be placed directly in the feeding bins on your factory floor without delay – again your vendor's responsibility. Wand-to-order material can be delivered directly to the Shop Floor in the consuming locations – and again your vendor's responsibility. NON-certified material cannot be interjected directly into your manufacturing process and becomes your responsibility to perform inspection and delivery to the point of use, along with all the necessary record keeping in between. Without certified vendors, many of the benefits gained by having agreements for the in-house store, the "Bread Man routine" and the Wand-to-order delivery systems are lost. Without certification it will be necessary for these vendors to deliver their material to your Inspection Department prior to it being injected into your manufacturing process. Many variables will be introduced into your procurement process, such as the ones caused by: rejections or the mere possibility of rejections, inspection times and delays, errors in inspection; you will be adding an additional class of material to your business – material awaiting inspection, additional record keeping activity, and all the inevitable errors that go with the additional record keeping. You will also have to add manpower to perform these inspections and stock clerks to take care of the additional material handling activities.

The key elements of a good vendor and component certification program are as follows:

- Certification is the process of examining a vendor's capabilities to gain reasonable assurance that the vendor has the ability to supply an acceptable quality product on a repeatable basis. Items to be reviewed and considered as evidence that a vendor can perform are as follows:

Certified Vendors

- Vendor performance history. A sample criterion of the minimum acceptable quality level for certification is: 98% of all material that has been delivered over the last 12 months has been acceptable.
- Evidence of the supplier's existing effective quality programs, such as Six Sigma or Statistical Process Control. Also, evidence that an effective corrective action program is in place.
- The vendor's recent quality history, both internal to his operation as well as with other Customers.
- Supplier quality survey – this can be an on- site audit or in some cases (depending on the type of components the supplier is expected to supply) the survey can be done remotely by mail or phone. For instance: If the vendor in question is being asked to supply common hardware or electronic components that he distributes, and the items he distributes are manufactured by reputable multinational corporations, you may elect to have vendors mail you the completed survey. On the other hand, if the vendor were being asked to manufacture several critical components to be fabricated in their factory, an on-site audit and survey would be appropriate.
- Certification should be reviewed at least annually.
- You may accept ISO certification as evidence that a vendor can perform to your satisfaction. If you accept ISO certification as evidence of a supplier's capability, you should request a copy of their certificate and assurances that you will be notified in the event the supplier loses their certification.
- The Sourcing, Quality and Manufacturing Engineering or Engineering organizations must unanimously agree and sign off on the supplier for the supplier to receive

certification. This is not a situation where the majority rules. All must unanimously agree to certify a vendor. If there are any dissenters, the vendor is not certified until corrective action can be taken that will satisfy each member of the certification Team.

- De-certification – your program should provide for de-certification in the event that the supplier's overall quality level drops below an acceptable level, say 95%. I am citing the 95% level as an example; the actual limits that will apply here and with the rest of your certification program will depend on the nature of your business and your own quality requirements.

  De-certification could also come about if the supplier certification was based on ISO certification and that certification is either cancelled or not renewed. In this situation the supplier should be de-certified in your program until he is either re-certified or achieves certification through your regular certification process.

A good supplier certification survey will contain the following elements:

- Supplier Information – supplier name, locations, size, business description and contact information, etc.
- A description of the types of items to be supplied.
- Plant and facility information – description of the plant size, processes performed, equipment and lead times, etc.
- Key personnel and their background.
- ISO certification information.
- Verification of processes and controls:
  - Inspection processes.
  - Drawing, specification, methods sheets and Engineering change controls.

- Floor worker diligence in the use of the proper documentation, tools, fixtures and equipment.
- Adequate control of equipment, including calibration (usually traceable to the National Institute of Standards and Technology).
- Preventative maintenance program in place.
- Proper identification of materials.
- Proper control of defective material and corrective action program, including follow-up.
- Proper storage and packaging controls.

Once you are satisfied that your supplier is ready for certification, the next step is to seal the bargain with a formal "Supplier Certification Agreement." This agreement will spell out the basis for certification; components to be covered; records retention; labeling requirements; quality levels the supplier is expected to maintain; what actions are expected in the event of non-conformance (reaction time, who pays for what, corrective action); lastly, de-certification levels and consequences. All parties should sign this agreement signifying their buy-in.

Once your supplier is certified, the next step is to certify each component that will be included in the agreement. Again, quality history is needed. If no history is available, then one will have to be established through the inspection process, starting with a first article inspection. As with vendor certification, component certification should be approved by Sourcing, Quality and Manufacturing Engineering or Engineering representatives. Again, nothing less than a unanimous opinion is acceptable.

As a point of clarification: Only a certified vendor can deliver a certified component. There are two separate and distinct yet related certification processes involved in a certification program. First is the vendor certification and second is the component certification. You can de-certify a component without de-certifying the vendor who supplies the component. A supplier's overall quality level is the combined quality level for all the different components he supplies. Therefore a supplier can remain at the 98% quality level, even though one of the components he supplies is de-certified because its quality level has slipped to the 90% level.

When an individual component is de-certified, all further receipts of the component must go through the incoming inspection process until the component certification process is repeated, either with the original vendor or a different replacement vendor.

It is a good idea to require that all material entering your facility be immediately identified as either certified material or material requiring inspection. Most business systems will perform this identification task automatically. It should be easy for anyone to determine the material's status as a certified or non-certified component, either by querying the business system or reviewing the material itself. Whatever process is used, it should ensure that non-certified materials never enter your manufacturing cells without first passing inspection.

Certified vendor and certified components are a must for optimizing the utilization of inventory assets. Again, bringing certified material into your facility eliminates the need for inventory to cover the queue time prior to inspection, the inspection time itself, the provision for a possible rejection, the queue time after inspection and the delivery time to the manufacturing cell. Also, all the time associated with the aforementioned is eliminated when you are taking delivery of certified parts from certified vendors, enhancing flexibility and velocity and allowing you to better meet your Customers' changing needs, thereby maximizing income.

Summary

Certification is the process of examining a vendor's capabilities to gain reasonable assurance that the vendor has the ability to supply an acceptable quality product on a repeatable basis. Among the considerations in determining a vendor's ability to meet your certification requirements will be the vendor's performance history; evidence of the supplier's existing effective quality programs; and a quality audit and survey. Also, you may accept ISO certification as evidence that a vendor can perform to your satisfaction.

A good certified vendor program will allow you to move material smoothly into your facility and directly to the manufacturing cell or point of use areas consuming the material. Your certified vendors can serve you well when they are delivering certified material in one of our three chosen delivery methods: The in-house store can deliver directly to the manufacturing cell. Material being delivered via the "Bread Man routine" will be placed directly in the feeding bins on your factory floor without delay. Wand-to-order material can be delivered directly to the Shop Floor in the consuming locations. NON-certified material cannot be interjected directly into your manufacturing process and becomes your responsibility to perform inspection and delivery to the point of use, along with all the necessary record keeping in between. Without certified vendors, many of the benefits gained by having agreements for the in-house store, the "Bread Man routine," and the Wand-to-order delivery systems are lost. Without certification it will be necessary for these vendors to deliver their material to your Inspection Department, prior to it being injected into your manufacturing process.

Certified vendor and certified components are a must for optimizing the utilization of inventory assets. Again, bringing certified material into your facility eliminates the need for inventory to cover the queue time prior to inspection, the inspection time itself, the provision for a possible rejection, the queue time after inspection and the delivery time to the manufacturing cell.

CHAPTER 12

Monitoring Labor Costs and Controlling Other Costs

Monitoring Labor Costs

Who Should Own the Cost Accounting Function

Okay, let's start out with a rather controversial concept. At least most accountants will think it is a controversial concept at first glance. However, on closer examination they should love the concept. Here it is: Place responsibility for Cost Accounting and all related functions in the Manufacturing Department, preferably in the Manufacturing Engineering arena. What better way to control costs than to make the Manufacturing operations leader the one responsible for measuring and analyzing his or her own costs? After all, real control of labor, material and equipment costs rests with the manufacturing folks, not with the Accountants. Responsibility, accountability and authority go together; you can't have one without the other two. I am not suggesting that Finance give up all controllership and oversight for manufacturing costs. I am in favor of strong controllership, but cooperative controllership with the acknowledgement that the main purpose is to assist the folks that create the value in the business – namely, the Manufacturing folks. I am suggesting that those folks responsible for Cost Accounting functions, or whatever your organization calls them, report solid line to the Manufacturing organization and dotted line to the Finance organization. I have successfully used this form of reporting for years. It has brought great understanding to the factory floor, leading to good solid cost Management in the manufacturing area.

Monitoring the Labor Costs

So in our new organization, how are we going to monitor labor costs without Work Orders? Easy — we use the time and attendance records to collect total labor hours for an area. This could be a product line, such as product "A" or a group of products, such as "sterile disposable products." Compare the total number of actual hours collected to the standard hours for the product or products produced times the number of products produced. The difference is over-absorbed or under-absorbed labor hours. Multiply this times the hourly rates and you have dollars over-absorbed or under-absorbed. In other words: If John and Jim worked a total of 80 hours to manufacture 20 widgets, each widget represents four actual labor hours. If the standard for the widget is five hours, labor is over-absorbed by one hour for each widget or a total over-absorption of 20 hours. If both John and Jim make $10.00 an hour, the labor is over-absorbed by a total of $200.00.

Of course, for the above to work you have to know what the standard time required to make a widget is. Your Manufacturing Engineering or Manufacturing folks can periodically monitor the assembly process to determine a fair standard. Allowances can be made for set up, breaks and personal time, etc. Analysis of actual trends will tell you when it is time to revisit the standard. More importantly, chronic and persistent occurrences of under-absorbed labor may be an indication of a process problem, material problems, equipment problems or other as yet undetected problems. These red flags should be investigated to root out and correct the process problems.

Using the Data

You should be using this data to ferret out problems with the manufacturing process. This data should not be used to persecute your Shop Floor workers. If you are having a problem with absorption and you cannot find a process problem, talk to your people. A good forum for such conversations is the daily or every other day cell meeting. These meetings should cover issues related to material, labor, equipment and quality – labor costs fit into this medium. Also, remember that the Shop Floor workers can request the presence of support staff at these meetings, such as personnel from Sourcing, Quality, Engineering, Cost Accounting or anyone that can contribute to the problem-solving process and process improvements. In the next Chapter we will discuss creating flexibility with labor.

Controlling Other Costs:

Where to Look for Cost Savings, and Labor Hours

Overtime reduction is a good area to look at for possible reduction. However, it also can be very profitable to work overtime. Provided you are getting a good hour's work during the overtime hours, it may actually cost you less to work overtime in some businesses. The overtime pay can cost less than hiring another full time employee when you consider the added costs to carry a new employee on your payroll, such as: health and dental insurance; life insurance; threshold 401k match; pension costs; vacation and holiday pay; costs for required environmental health and safety training; costs for other job-related training. These are some of the costs you don't have to incur when your employees work overtime. If you find that you are working too many overtime hours and this is causing either poor productivity or a truly higher hourly cost after taking the above into consideration, then by all means add more workers to your work force.

Also, use your standard cost system to determine whether overtime has become a habit. If you have a good cost system in place, it should be easy to detect a lower output rate per hour. Of course, the opposite is true, the same or higher output per hour gives assurance that overtime is required. The proper use of overtime is necessary to create the flexibility for labor we need in operating our continuous flow factory. It is important that it be managed carefully and not be abused.

Temporary workers and contractors have their place in a flexible factory. They can help reduce the number of required overtime hours. Temps and contractors can be less costly than adding regular employees because they usually do not enjoy the same expensive benefits regular workers do. The same goes for part-timers; they usually don't share in benefit programs to the same extent as regular employees, making them cost less. But don't forget to constantly reassess their need. Also, remember that it is easier and less costly to layoff this type of employee. They understand their position with the company is not permanent.

It may be possible to eliminate an entire shift. If you are working two or three shifts and can cut one of the shifts out completely, you will save the overhead costs associated with running another shift. Some of these costs are shift supervision; heat and air-conditioning; additional security; additional maintenance.

Process improvements to remove labor provide excellent opportunities for cost reductions. Eliminating rework is high on this list. Improving yields net all the labor in the items that would have either been scrapped or reworked. Work simplification usually results in labor cost savings. Also, outsourcing items that can be contracted to an outside vendor for a lower cost is a great way to save, provided it would not affect your throughput velocity.

Any item that does not fit your core competency should be considered for outsourcing.

Equipment Leases

Review all equipment leases for opportunity. Look at copiers, shipping dock equipment, trucks, cars and storage trailers. A better deal may be available now for your current or expiring leases. The equipment being leased may no longer be necessary; if this is so, return it. This is especially true with storage trailers; once on your property, they tend to be used, needed or not. If the material stored in these trailers is obsolete, get rid of it and return the trailers. The same applies to offsite storage facility leases. The key to controlling these costs is a constant review and justification for keeping the lease open. It may be less costly at some point to buy out a lease than to continue leasing. Leases have a tendency to become evergreen; they just go on and on forever, earning the green for the leaser.

Services

Review items like carpets, alarm systems, fire extinguishers, sprinkler system servicing and phone-related services like music to make sure you are getting the most for your dollar. Equipment servicing for things like fork trucks, bailers, dock lifters and other machinery should be reviewed regularly. Assign someone to watch over these expenses and review them on a regular basis. Almost every company of significant size has some sort of service expense they are paying for that is either no longer needed or can be replaced with an alternate, less expensive method. These are expenses that get forgotten in the busy day-to-day running of a business.

Scrap Costs

Eliminating scrap costs is essential. In the 1960s a company could survive with even a 10% defect rate. However, in the 1970s defect rates fell below 10% and in the early 1980s world competition demanded defect rates of less than 1%. From 1985 forward the target has been zero defects and it is not uncommon to hear of defects being measured in parts per million, as with Six Sigma quality levels, which are 3.4 DPMO (defects per million opportunities). It is obvious that a company with a 5% scrap rate today is in serious trouble, and there still are manufacturing facilities generating scrap at these levels in some areas.

In addition to the direct material cost and the labor and overhead that went into the scrapped item, scrap can reduce your top line through lost revenue. High rates of internal scrap usually also show up as latent failures in the form of Out-of-Box Failures. These are the worst failures because your Customers find them for you when they first go to use your product. If a Customer only buys one item from you and that item is defective, everything he has ever bought from you is no good. He will be reluctant to try your product again.

Increased warranty cost is usually directly related to a high rate of scrap. When you are generating a high rate of scrap, your process is out of control. As a consequence, even the material that passes for good material can be compromised. Sooner or later that material will probably show up as a defect somewhere, if not in your factory, as an Out-of-Box Failure and/or warranty expense with your Customer.

Many rules have their exceptions. One business I was connected with sold a warranty that assured a Customer that he would be supplied with a sensor for a period of time, one year for one price, two years for another higher price and three years for a still higher price. As an example, let's say the item with a 30-day warranty was sold for around $100.00. The item with a one-year warranty was sold for $1,000 dollars. The item cost $18 dollars to make. The warranty was for a no questions asked replacement, as many as needed during the year. If the Customer did not use any replacements in the year, he would receive a $300 credit toward the next year's extension that cost another $1,000 dollars. If it had not been for the fact that these sensors experienced common failures, it would not have been possible to sell these warranty plans. A few things to remember: first, the product quality was on par with the competition; second, these circumstances are very rare. Unless you find yourself in a similar situation, you had better eliminate your scrap, Out-of-Box Failures and warranty expenses. They are all closely related.

Supplies

There are two sides to reducing these expenses. Get the best price you can for items like (electro static discharge) shop coats, but remember the purpose is to reduce latent failures of sensitive electronic components and equipment. Small tools can usually be added to an in-house store agreement. Don't skimp on small tools. I knew of situations where employees were waiting for another employee to finish with a small hand tool so they could use the same tool because there was only one in the area. This kind of nonsense is pure waste but is still seen all too often.

Utilities

Phones – good shopping for the correct plan and equipment usually pays off. Here the scene is changing all the time. Stay on top of the changes and offerings, but don't disrupt your business to save a few pennies. Cell phones and pagers are prolific. They can be great tools; however, these items can become a status symbol rather than a business tool. Everyone will want one for the status that goes with the device. Guard against this by really justifying their need before handing them out. The best way to administer these items is to let the employee sign up for a personal plan in their own name and then allow the company calls as an expense. This also means the company picks up only the portion of the minimum that was used for company business.

Electricity, water and gas also provide opportunities for cost savings. In one operation I was with, energy was over seven percent of the total product cost. A third shift was added for high power testing, primarily to take advantage of the lower electric rates in the late evening and early morning hours. Boilers that can run on both gas and oil can produce savings by using the fuel that is the cheapest when you are buying and switching back and forth between fuels when necessary.

Depreciation

Unneeded assets that can be transferred or sold should be. If not, they will continue to take up valuable floor space and may even require maintenance or periodic calibration. If the unused equipment is considered to be in service, it will be on the preventative maintenance schedule, which means it will be receiving periodically scheduled maintenance. The same is true for equipment needing calibration; it will be sucking up technical resources to calibrate a piece of equipment no longer needed. Also, your depreciation list should be reviewed to ferret out non-existent assets that have been disposed of and not removed from the asset list. Do these things routinely to reduce your depreciations expense.

Freight

This area is usually loaded with low hanging fruit. Look for vendors with several freight charges on the same day. Charging freight for multiple deliveries when several items arrived in the same package is a common error suppliers make. Do not pay for freight on items carried in your in-house store, and the same goes for the "Bread Man routine" items. Buyers should try to get the supplier to pay for delivery. When you do pay for freight, make sure you agreed to pay this charge. When you ship, make sure you ship for the lowest cost for the required service. Sensitize your own folks to the abuses of shipping overnight when it is not really necessary. These are only a few suggestions to get the ball rolling. As you take smaller and smaller deliveries more frequently, freight charges will take on more significance and require better Management.

Calibration

As mentioned above, equipment not in service should be formally removed from service to prevent unnecessary calibration. This can require one last calibration to prove that the last items calibrated using this equipment were being calibrated to build specification. Analyze your calibration costs to determine whether it is better to do your own calibration or employ an outside service.

Other areas to explore for cost savings that may be over- looked are:

- Housekeeping costs, including the cost of space used to store obsolete items.
- Dispose of obsolete items early to produce the biggest return on the sale. Age will rarely enhance the value of obsolete items.
- Product packaging costs can yield nice savings. Be on the lookout for new revolutionary packaging methods. Some of the newer packaging methods are environmentally friendly as well as cost effective.
- Travel and entertainment costs can be reviewed for reductions. Be careful here; do not forget to celebrate successes – even small ones.
- Discretionary meetings can be cut altogether or held "in company" rather than at a local hotel.
- Identify Shop Floor space you pay for and maybe don't use. Isolate it, close it off, and turn off the lights and air conditioning.
- Assign expenses that are allocated over several areas of responsibility to an owner. If nobody feels responsible for

these expenses, the likelihood of them being optimized is slim.

- Review decisions to make or purchase items such as CDs and manuals. Changes in technology may make it profitable to perform certain tasks in-house that you are currently outsourcing. One example is the CD that is shipped as documentation with your product. Current technology makes it not only cost effective to make in-house, it can be a logistics as well as an inventory advantage, especially when many different versions of the software are required.

Although many of the costs discussed here are not necessarily part of the direct product cost, they can still have a significant impact on overall costs. A key to controlling these costs is not to lose sight of them. Add to this list your own set of costs that need controlling and review them on a regular basis.

Summary

One of the most effective ways to control costs is to make the Manufacturing operations leader the one responsible for measuring and analyzing his or her own costs. After all, real control of labor, material and equipment costs rests with the manufacturing folks, not with the accountants. Responsibility, accountability and authority go together; you can't have one without the other two.

You can use the time and attendance records to collect total labor hours and your production records to collect actual output for a given area. Comparing this to the established standard hours for the output will allow you to monitor your area for output effectiveness. This data will help point the way toward problems with the manufacturing process. More importantly, chronic and persistent occurrences of under-absorbed labor may be an indication of a process problem, material problem, equipment

Monitoring Labor Costs and Controlling Other Costs

problem or other as yet undetected problems. These red flags should be investigated to root out and correct any process problems.

Other costs that require attention in order to maximize the bang for your buck are: overtime expenses, equipment leases, outside services, scrap costs, supplies, utilities, depreciation, freight, maintenance and calibration, housekeeping, obsolete material, product packaging, travel and entertainment, and floor space. A key to controlling these costs is not to lose sight of them. Assign a responsible party to monitor and manage each of these costs.

CHAPTER 13

Creating Equipment Flexibility

Capacity

In most cases, overall equipment flexibility as it relates to capacity is a given. The majority of companies are working one eight-hour shift, five days a week, augmented by a small amount of overtime when necessary. This means that the equipment is sitting idle 16 hours a day during the five-day work week and 24 hours a day on most weekends. There is a great deal of capacity and flexibility in that idle time.

To continue the cost of overtime discussion started in the last chapter: The extra labor cost to take advantage of the additional capacity on an overtime basis is much less than you would think, at first glance. If you are paying your employees time and a half after the first forty hours (or after eight hours in a day in some cases), this cost for overtime is almost a wash in most companies and can even be less costly in others. When you compare the cost of overtime to the cost of adding new people, overtime can look pretty inexpensive. First, you have benefits such as medical insurance, dental insurance, life insurance, 401K matches, pension expense, etc. In many companies these add up to 40% or more of the base pay. Second, often you are not paying for break time when employees work overtime. If an employee works one or two hours overtime, they usually don't take any additional breaks. Third, there are no additional training costs associated with the folks that work overtime. Your overtime workers already know how to do their jobs. They are the same reliable workers that are already building your products during the regular work day. When you consider all the required training – not only the training associated with the building of your product, but also other required training such as environmental health and safety training — the training bill can be huge. Fourth, you save on backroom expenses such as Payroll, Accounting, Human Resource record maintenance, employment taxes, etc. Last but not least, you usually pick the most reliable and productive workers to work overtime, so you should get the best on an overtime basis. Even if you have a Union Shop and are required to rotate overtime, the best workers are usually the ones that want the extra work, and the ones with less energy usually turn down the overtime. Of course, all these savings are based on you getting an equally productive hour's work on an overtime basis as you do on a regular hourly basis. There is a balance to be struck here. You should add people if you find that you are working your people excessive amounts of overtime for months at a time.

In addition to or in place of the overtime solution, you can add a shift. Adding a shift allows you to take advantage of your existing equipment. Usually the only increase in Management expense is for any necessary additional direct supervision for the new shift. However, additional employees will create the added expenses we were saving in our discussion above by working overtime, such as additional insurances and training, etc.

Adding Equipment

There are opportunities to create flexibility by adding equipment or duplicating equipment in the production cells. I can't believe the number of times that I have witnessed one operator waiting for another operator to finish with an inexpensive hand tool or power tool so that he or she could use the same tool. This is

Creating Equipment Flexibility

an area where a skilled Manufacturing Engineer can really earn his or her keep by finding the optimum tool and equipment solutions. Better yet, train all your people to look for opportunities like this. There will be more about training coming up in the next Chapter.

Earlier I cited the examples of adding a dedicated ultrasonic welder to a work cell. In this case the addition of the welder eliminated an operator carrying work across the factory to an ultrasonic welder in another cell, necessitating a change in set up and the waste of material in adjusting for the set up. However, the biggest savings came not in the set-up time savings or the travel to and from the other cell, but in the inventory savings by eliminating the need to make the welded assemblies in batches. With the welder right in the cell where the assemblies were consumed, they could be welded in line as needed. The equipment was always set up.

Another example mentioned earlier was the addition of a hot stamping machine. By adding this machine to the production cell, the outsourcing of the assembly for the marking operation was eliminated. This saved days of inventory time as well as shipping and handling costs, not to mention the paperwork moving the assembly in and out of the facility. This was one of the action items that enabled this product to be started and completed and stocked in the same day.

In another factory of mine we added a Bridgeport miller to the mechanical components fabrication area, eliminating the need to send a component to the Machine Shop at the other end of the factory. Again, this eliminated the need to manufacture in batch lots, as the parts could effectively be made as needed right in the consuming department.

An excellent example of gaining flexibility by combining equipment took place in a Connecticut factory in the early 1970s. The idea was to merge a final assembly cell that manufactured x-ray equipment with a pack-and-ship cell. The number of possible combinations for a final product manufactured in this facility, including its accessories, was well over 10,000 possibilities. The problem was how to provide for same day delivery of all combinations of product without maintaining huge inventories. The solution was to finish building the product in the Shipping Department to each Customer's request. The President of this company hired me, as he said, to make his Shipping Department look like the supermarket across the street. Clearly this man was way ahead of his time, given that we are talking about the early '70s. When you think about it, you realize that the flow-manufacturing factory is like a combination of the American grocery store and Henry Ford's assembly line. The end result was a pack-and-ship-area that did the final assembly of the finished product. Assembly equipment was moved into the shipping area along with all the individual components that together made up the 10,000 possible combinations. Items that created the variations were several types of filters, end covers, heat exchangers, fans, several cable lengths, different mounting devices, collimating devices and finally colors. Even a paint booth and baking station were constructed to over spray each unit with the custom colors ordered by the Customers. The product was shipped the same day the Customer's Order was received. Combining the final assembly function with the shipping function in one department and relocating the equipment from the Final Assembly Departments and a few other areas created the flexibility to gain a competitive edge – the ability to deliver to the Customer the same day when the competition couldn't.

Similarly, adding automatic cut off saws to a raw material warehouse created the flexibility needed to eliminate many different sizes of bar stock. This saved thousands of dollars in raw material inventory and allowed for control of some exotic materials. The components being manufactured required an "oxygen-free copper" because they were being used inside a vacuum device. If the components were made from regular copper, the

Creating Equipment Flexibility

finished product was useless and would have to be scrapped at a cost of several thousand dollars for each of several units affected. The oxygen that would be emitted from the regular copper component when the vacuum device was powered up would render it inoperable and un-repairable. Controlling the raw material in a controlled warehouse by cutting the "oxygen free copper" to size, then sending it to the machining centers to be machined into components ensured that the components would function correctly in a vacuum. Adding the automatic cut off saws not only reduced inventory by permitting the material to be cut to any size, it also provided a measure of control over the material being used in manufacturing the product.

New ways of thinking for equipment operators are sometimes required when adding new machinery that increases flexibility. Adding a machining center with automatic pallet changers and tool changers to an in-house Machine Shop in one of our factories enabled us to bring functions inside our facility that had previously been subcontracted to outside vendors. Flexibility was created by eliminating all the queuing and manufacturing time necessary for the outside vendors to do their portion of the machining. This allowed the bill-of-materials to be flattened, eliminating several levels and all the associated transactions necessary when building the product. Remember, one key objective in a flow manufacturing facility is to keep the item you are manufacturing progressing through your factory without interruption. This is a tough goal to achieve whenever you find it necessary to start working on a component or assembly and in mid-stream send the item outside your facility for further processing, then bring it back for further work inside your facility. To get back to the operator: when the operator was first introduced to his new machine, he would shut the equipment down during his coffee breaks. On a visit to this area, seeing the machine idle, I asked the operator if the machine was down for repair. He told me: "Oh no, I am on my coffee break." After I asked him if he thought the

Winning in a Highly Competitive Manufacturing Environment

machine needed a break too, the light came on. The machine was not privileged to any future coffee breaks from that day on.

In another situation, a piece of equipment that tested the quality of a type of film used in medical imaging devices was relocated to an area where disposable medical products were manufactured. Moving the equipment increased flexibility by allowing the dedicated quality assurance people monitoring the clean room functions to also perform the film testing functions. The natures of both job functions were such that they could be accomplished concurrently. This move not only allowed for the elimination of a dedicated film tester but also provided further flexibility by having several trained folks readily available to perform the film testing procedure when backup was required.

Being innovative with equipment to create flexibility can be a very rewarding and satisfying experience for all who are involved. A group of Manufacturing and Manufacturing Engineering folks were consolidating and improving a film winding business in Connecticut from one location in Germany and another in California. Again, this was a medical imaging film product used in the cardio-vascular arena. The short version is this: we purchased very large rolls of film in large quantity and converted them into very small rolls of film (the winding operation), then packaged the film for Customers to use in a hospital environment, shipping the film with the appropriate developer. The work had to be done in total darkness, no light whatsoever, and in a cool dry environment. There were five rooms in California and one in Germany. 14 people were devoted to the manufacturing end of the business in Germany and California combined and they were working a lot of overtime. After the move to Connecticut, the entire manufacturing function was accomplished with six people and they usually only worked on film winding three or four days a week. Only on rare occasions did the operation require a fifth day of operation. The innovation:

Creating Equipment Flexibility

- In Connecticut all the winding was done in one room – not six as was the case in Germany and California combined.
- A revolving door that did not allow any light to enter permitted the operators to come and go without having to shut the operation down. Previously the individual rooms had to be shut down and the product had to be sealed away to protect it from the light when the door was opened to permit entry and exit for any reason.
- Interlocking feeding doors were installed to allow raw film to be fed into the room on one side and finished product to be passed out of the room on the other side. Again this permitted a continuous operation when bringing material into and removing material from the room. This had not been the case prior to the move.
- Automatic cutters were installed on the rolling equipment, making this operation easy to perform in total darkness.

There were other innovative changes that made the winding tasks easier to perform in the dark. The employees that worked in the darkroom were all volunteers; most suffered from migraine headaches and claimed the cool, dark, dry environment helped with their headaches. They were happy to be there and were very productive. Unfortunately, we had more volunteers than we had need of. The people involved with this transition had a lot of fun with this very successful project. Long after the room was up and running in full production, they continued to make innovative improvements with equipment and methods.

Another very successful Team using innovative ideas to improve equipment and processes operated as a Cross-Functional Self-Directed Team in the disposables area of the same business. The end result of the Team's efforts was a 30% reduction in floor space, a 50% reduction in work-in-process inventory and a direct labor reduction of 1,500 hours a month, which represented more than 25% of the total available monthly hours in this department.

As a side note, these people did not lose their jobs as a result of their efforts to reduce labor hours. Excessive overtime had been worked in this area as well as other areas of this factory. As these employees were cross-trained to perform several functions in other areas of the business, they were used to reduce the need for overtime. As a result, the 1,500 hours was absorbed. Working a fair amount of overtime in your facility gives you the flexibility to absorb the excess labor that results from this kind of innovation. All you have to do is replace some of the overtime with the excess labor created, provided you have a well cross-trained workforce, which is the subject of the next Chapter. The innovations:

- Adding a new crimping press to perform a crimping operation that had previously been done by hand.
- Adding a semi-automatic grinder with a vacuum device for plastic chip removal.
- Installing new benches with more electrical and air line drops.
- Automated test equipment was added that eliminated the need for frequent calibration of the old test beds previously used to test the product.
- Label dispensing equipment that properly placed the labels quickly.
- Automatic dispensers for epoxies that ensured quick application of the correct amount of epoxy.
- A vacuum pump to automatically remove solutions from a cartridge assembly during the production process.

Along with the equipment additions and changes, the sterilization process was modified. This required extensive validation testing to prove that the new protocol being used was effective. The idea was to be able to mix like items together when sterilizing the final product. This would permit full utilization of the sterilization facilities while allowing smaller quantities of the product to be sterilized at the same time. Rather than sterilizing the required 1,000 cases of product "Q" and 1,000 cases of product "R" in two separate loads, product "Q" and "R" could be sterilized together. This meant that it was necessary to sterilize only one load containing 500 cases of product "Q" and 500 cases of product "R." This produced great inventory savings. Again, my people on this Team had a great deal of fun meeting these challenges.

Swapping Equipment

Replacing old equipment with automated equipment can pay off big. One example is replacing printed circuit board component locators with random component locators. The earlier models of component locators had a series of bins that progressed in sequence to an opening in the tabletop surface. An overhead light would shine on the location on the raw circuit board where the component was to be placed. The bins and the light were synchronized so that when the light shone on an area, the bin containing the correct component would be exposed in the table top for easy access. Setting these machines up was cumbersome and time consuming. The next generation of equipment was the random component locator. The advantage of these newer machines was that the bins would appear randomly as preprogrammed. This meant that the same components would remain in the same bins for all boards manufactured on this particular machine, eliminating the bin set up. On occasion it would be necessary to change an entire set of bins for another series of boards. The neat thing was that you could make similar types of boards on the same machine without changing the set up. The operators could use the keyboard to key in the board number they wanted to populate and only the right bins for that board would appear when the light shone on the holes the component went in. The random component locator could be programmed for the assembly of several different boards. With three or four machines you could assemble dozens of different types of boards without ever changing the part set ups. This basic concept for through hole boards is in common use today.

Another and even greater advancement for the assembly of circuit boards is the surface mount board. Machines that populate these boards can lay down thousands of components per hour. They are very complex and expensive pieces of equipment, some costing hundreds of thousands of dollars. Parts can be set up on carriages, shortening set up time dramatically. Even though this equipment is very expensive, board reliability and the reduction of component cost are great enough in many instances to warrant the investment.

In one of my factories I replaced older test equipment that was used to test medical equipment functionality by simulating patient conditions. It was necessary to document the testing by printing and storing the test results in a "device history folder." These folders were one half to one inch thick, filled with test documentation for each monitor manufactured. This test equipment was replaced with test equipment that downloaded the product history test results automatically onto a server. This eliminated the thick "device history folders" and all the costs associated with creating, maintaining and storing them.

Another closely related event involved the destruction of a central burn-in oven that required all equipment with a burn-in specification to be transported to the central oven. This large oven was replaced with many smaller ovens that were placed in or near the manufacturing cell for each product.

Improving Equipment

Improving existing equipment can be driven through your Shop Floor Teams. Mistake proofing your processes will lead to equipment improvements. One area for improvement was found in the cable assembly area. During the introduction of

Statistical Process Control (SPC), capability studies were conducted to determine each piece of equipment's ability to manufacture a good quality product on a repeatable basis. Almost every connector-staking machine was found to be unreliable. Either there was a problem with the tooling or the chosen connector for the wire or the calibration of the machine. Cables are not sexy devices and engineers do not tend to labor over their design, hence it is an area ripe for finding low hanging fruit. The tooling was repaired or replaced. The correct machine was selected for the correct process and SPC charts were created to continually monitor the process. Reliability and cost were both greatly improved. Prior to this effort, many of the problems were not found until the unit failed final test. This is the most costly place inside your factory to find defects. Units would fail test (some units went through two hours of testing before failing) and at that point a Technician would be required to troubleshoot and repair the unit. The success of this endeavor, along with similar efforts, increased first-pass yield – measured by the number of units that passed test the first time without any rework – from 42% to over 99%.

Moving Equipment

The simple task of examining the location of equipment within your facility can lead to increased efficiency. In one of the factories that I was converting to flow manufacturing there was a lot of equipment devoted to manufacturing sensors. The simple act of diagraming the flow of the product through the facility revealed a ridiculously circuitous route for one series of sensors. The equipment had been used to manufacture a type of sensor that had become obsolete and was no longer manufactured. However, it never occurred to anybody to combine all the equipment for the new sensor in one area to eliminate queue time, travel time and batch building. The equipment was moved into one cell, reducing inventory and improving velocity and quality.

If copiers or printers are used in the manufacturing process, then get them out of the offices and on the factory floor. Also, if scales are needed, move those scales onto the Shop Floor. Be sure there are plenty of electrical drops available. If water or drains are required, see that they are in the work area. Hand tools and fixtures should be close by. If transactions are done in the work cell, have scanners and/or terminals close by in the cell. If bar codes are printed in the manufacturing process, have bar code printers in the cell. Bench and cell design is so important to your success. Your manufacturing cells should always be under review for improvement.

The above are just a few examples; the possibilities are virtually endless. The best way to pursue these issues is to involve your Shop Floor workers through their cell Team meetings, using your Manufacturing Engineering or related group to screen, encourage and guide the process.

Summary

Overall equipment flexibility as it relates to capacity is a given in the majority of companies who are working one eight-hour shift, five days a week, augmented by a small amount of overtime when necessary. This means that the equipment is sitting idle 16 hours a day during the five-day work week and 24 hours a day on most weekends. There is a great deal of capacity and flexibility in that idle time. This capacity can be unlocked by working overtime or by adding one or two entire shifts.

Innovating with equipment to create flexibility can be very profitable for your business and a very satisfying experience for all who are involved. You can employ techniques such as adding equipment to increase flexibility and capacity; replacing old equipment with automated equipment; relocating equipment and their functions; and combining equipment from several different cells into one common cell. These equipment utilization methods can increase flexibility and eliminate the need to build

Creating Equipment Flexibility

in batch lots, thereby reducing your inventory, increasing velocity and improving quality. These types of projects are fun and exciting opportunities for your Manufacturing Engineering staff and "Self-Directed Teams" to work on. Also, don't forget to involve your Shop Floor workers through their cell Team meetings, using your Manufacturing Engineers to screen, encourage and guide the process.

CHAPTER 14

Creating Labor Flexibility Through Training

As previously discussed, there is a certain amount of labor flexibility inherent in any operation that is not working three full shifts, seven days a week. You can always work overtime, adding to your total available hours. This overtime is not as costly as it first appears. However, we will not be concentrating on this type of flexibility here. The type of flexibility we will be focusing on in this chapter is that flexibility which we gain from having a well cross-trained workforce. In one of my more recent factories it was not unheard of to have an employee making circuit boards in the morning, building treadmills in the afternoon, and the next day that same employee could be either testing fetal monitors or winding medical imaging film in a darkroom. This factory was a Union shop, so no excuses on that score. Gaining the support of the Union is simply a function of negotiating away many of the unnecessary labor grades and job classifications. This is the type of flexibility you will need, if you are going to maintain a velocity of three days or better with little inventory. And you need to maintain a velocity of three days or better, if you are going to be a world-class organization, satisfying your Customer's ever changing needs. Remember, if you don't satisfy your Customer's needs, your competition will. If you have no competitors to worry about today, and you don't satisfy your Customer's needs, you soon will have competitors and they will satisfy your Customer's needs.

Reward For Skills Learned

One way to encourage your employees to learn new skills is to make it profitable for them to learn new skills. One way this can be done is by basing pay grades or hourly rates on the number of skills sets an employee has accomplished. After all, the more an employee knows, the more valuable he or she is to the organization. Rather than paying a person for the skill level they are currently performing at and locking them into one task or set of skills, you pay them for all the skills they have mastered. This gives you the option to use them wherever their skills are most needed at any given moment, thereby creating greater flexibility for your organization. When you are paying employees for all the skills they have mastered, you and your Management Team will tend to more readily move these learned workers to the jobs where they are most needed to satisfy current demand. This moves you away from the mode of building inventory, just so you can keep your people (who only know how to perform tasks that have no current demand) occupied. Creating inventory just to keep them busy is counter-productive.

If you truly have no work other than building inventory, send those people to the cafeteria, buy them coffee and give them a deck of cards. Give them anything to do other than just building inventory. If this is a regular problem in your business, then you have too many people. Keeping too many people on the payroll does no one a favor. The amount of work available always has a tendency to expand to consume the number of labor hours available to do the work. If you have 35 hours of work and 40 hours of labor available, somehow the 35 hours of work will take 40 hours. The only way to win at this game is to make sure that you always have less labor available than is needed, then work a modest

Creating Labor Flexibility Through Training

amount of overtime to make up for any shortage of labor. Also, when there are more people than you need in your factory, these folks will find a way to amuse themselves. This does not always result in a positive experience for the company or the employee. Look for excess labor problems in areas of your business where employees are frequently bickering.

There are many ways to encourage your employees to learn the various skills they will need in your new Millennium Company. Recognition for mastering new skills or completion of a training program can take several forms such as job promotions, certificates, luncheons honoring the achievements, announcements, articles in the company or local newspaper, cash awards, etc. These can all be powerful motivators. Talk up training. Make sure your people understand that training is a valuable benefit, an investment the company is making in them personally, which provides a measure of job protection. Communicate that the training enhances their value in the overall job marketplace. Explain that they are responsible for and should take charge of their own career. You can provide the opportunity and encouragement, but they must put forth the effort and energy to execute well.

It is never easy to close a factory and move the work to a low cost country. However, it happens with regularity these days. If you have a highly trained workforce, they will be in high demand and this will be their best chance to find new work quickly. I moved a factory from Connecticut to Bangalore, India. The workforce in Connecticut was highly trained. In addition to the normal job skills they took with them, they were Six Sigma trained and had used Statistical Process Control manufacturing techniques for years. These workers were fully trained in flow manufacturing techniques and each employee had received extensive Poka-yoke (mistake proofing) training. Our employees were in such high demand that several area employers ran job fairs in our facility in an attempt to convince these highly trained workers to sign up with them for jobs when our plant finally closed. It wasn't very long after the plant closed before virtually everyone who wanted a job had one, even in a very tough job market. Many of these folks were able to bank their bonuses and severance pay and return to work right away. Knowing this sure helps one to sleep better at night.

Flow Manufacturing Makes Training More Important

The closer a factory moves toward flow manufacturing, the more important labor flexibility becomes. To react to Customer demand, the available labor will have to be able to perform the tasks required in filling the current orders, no matter what they are. Customer orders will rarely arrive in the mix that exactly complements the skill sets of your available labor, unless there is enough flexibility built into your labor force to meet almost any possible combination of demands. You may correctly forecast monthly sales of 400 of product "A" and 400 of product "B," but the orders may arrive for 200 of product "A" during the first and last week of the month and 200 of product "B" during the second and third week of the month. If only half your labor force had the skills necessary to build product "A" and the other half had only the skills necessary to build product "B," then during the first and forth weeks of the month when you only had orders for product "A," the half of the workforce that only had the skills necessary to build product "B" would be idle. Also during the second and third weeks of the month, the workers who had only the skills necessary to build product "A" would be idle. Further, assuming you had enough total labor available to build only 800 total units during the month, you would not have the necessary available product to satisfy either Customer in a timely manner because half your labor would be idle during the entire month. This is a very simple scenario. Of course, in real life there are usually many more than two products, and the orders arrive even more

Creating Labor Flexibility Through Training

erratically than illustrated in this scenario, making the necessity for labor flexibility even more important.

In several of my factories, adding various well-trained Management and staff employees to the available touch labor pool during peak demand periods enhanced flexibility. Everybody seemed to enjoy the change of pace brought about by an opportunity to actually help build the product. The Manufacturing Engineers, Quality folks and Supervisors got some good hands-on experience, which often led to positive changes in design and manufacturing methods, or at least to a better appreciation of the touch labor activities. The touch labor folks got a chance to harass the Management in a friendly and playful way. The pizza was always on the company and the drinks were always soft and plentiful. On many occasions employees were encouraged to take dinner home from the company cafeteria. This appeased the spouses, who were either home waiting for their dinner or relieved that they didn't have to cook dinner when their spouse arrived home late from work. Again, this was done in a Union shop. Remember, for twenty-two years I operated in a Union factory environment. I always had a deal with the Union that went like this: as long as I was offering unlimited overtime to all employees, non-union employees were allowed to pitch in. If your Union is stricter, there is usually always a deal you can work out, provided you have excellent relations with your Union. Excellent relations with your Union start with a mutual respect and will be only as good as the relations you have with your employees.

Simple Matrix

A simple matrix can be used to manage skill levels for your employees. Each manager should create and maintain a matrix with the names of the employees they are responsible for down the left side of the page and the different job functions or skill sets performed in their area across the top. An X is placed across from the employee's name and under the skill set that the employee has mastered. The manager's job is to encourage each employee to master as many skills as practically possible. Post the matrix in a very visible place for all to see. There is nothing like creating a little peer pressure and competition to get the ball rolling. The matrix must be well maintained or it will lose its effectiveness. Jobs in other areas of the factory not directly included in the Manager's area of responsibility should be included on the matrix. This will enable Managers to draw from other pools of trained labor when they have high labor demands and vice versa. All direct supervisors should work on completing the matrixes together to ensure cross-fertilization. Goals can be established, such as: all employees should know how to do at least three distinct jobs by the end of the year. Each Supervisor should also be measured and rewarded, based on how well he or she does at cross training their employees.

Full Time Trainer

If your organization can afford it, a full time trainer can prove to be a very valuable addition to your facility, and I don't see how you can not afford to add a full time trainer if you have more than one hundred employees. In today's business environment, with all the required EHS (Environmental Health and Safety) training, as well as required training by other Governmental organizations, it is almost a must to have a full time trainer on site, and he or she will certainly pay their own way many times over. The training is going to be done one way or the other, so why not have a professional maximize on the opportunity? In addition to the EHS training, the trainer can cover new employee orientation, HR training such as harassment training, ESD (static control) courses, Management development, ISO training, mistake proofing, computer skills, and flow manufacturing skills, as well as basic manufacturing skills such as: soldering techniques, component identification, blueprint reading, automated assembly, cycle counting, etc. In addition, your trainer can maintain the

Creating Labor Flexibility Through Training

necessary compliance records of the training that are required by so many Government and quasi-Government organizations.

My Trainers have been involved in all of the above training efforts. They became trusted members of our Team, keeping records of the skills each employee had mastered and scheduling employees for regularly scheduled refresher courses. If they had a course scheduled in soldering techniques with only three employees scheduled to attend, and there was room for eight in the class, they would post a notice on the classroom door offering the course to any volunteer that wanted to learn the skill they were teaching – in this case soldering techniques. We encouraged any employee who wanted to take the course to do so on our time. The classes were usually always full. The trainer can also pitch in during peak periods when an extra pair of hands is needed in any of the many areas he or she has expertise in.

In my factories, the Trainers were also tied into our Out-of-Box Failure process. The process called for the return and in-depth analysis of all field failures that were within 90 days of the ship date. The failures were broken down into four categories: First, random component failures – a purchased component like a resistor or capacitor would fail without any historical pattern indicating that there was a possibility of a failure. Second, Engineering failures – these were failures that could have been prevented had we had a more robust design. Third, no problem found – these were units that exhibited no problem when analyzed in our factory and usually indicated the Customer needed more training. The fourth, and most relevant in this discussion, were workmanship errors – these were problems that were caused by poor workmanship in our factory during the product manufacturing process. When the type of workmanship problem was determined, we could back track through the automated data collection system, using the unit's serial number to access the unit's data history file, in order to determine which operator was most likely the cause of the problem. This was done not with the intention of placing blame, but with the intention of further training to prevent future problems of this type. This is where the Trainer got involved. He would schedule the employee for the necessary training. Great care should be exercised here not to humiliate the employees involved. They must be made to understand that your intentions are solely to have the best-trained workforce possible and this is all part of the program.

Some of the types of training we offered in this factory were as follows:
- Flow manufacturing
- Component identification
- Soldering skills
- Surface mount repair
- Film winding in a dark room
- Fork truck driving
- Electronic Data collection
- Circuit board testing
- SPC Statistical Process Control
- Poka-yoke – mistake proofing
- ESD static control
- Print reading
- Automated assembly and test techniques
- FDA Good Manufacturing Practices
- Enterprise Resource Planning
- Bar coding
- Inventory Control and Cycle Counting
- EHS training
  - Hazardous waste

- Fire
- Lifting
- Ergonomics
- Proper storage
- HR training
  - Integrity
  - Harassment
  - Ethics
- Six Sigma training
  - Production Associates
  - Managers
- PC skills

The above examples were culled from a list of skills that were used to demonstrate to a group of employees in a company-wide meeting that they were the best-trained workforce in the State of Connecticut. It was important for these employees to understand what great assets they possessed in the skills they had developed over the years they had served their Company. They were valuable and valued employees. Understanding this value would drive them to learn even more to further insure that they would always be marketable employees. Our philosophy was, "Why would we want an employee on our payroll that nobody else wanted?" Sure we lost some of our best to other area employers, but very few left us. Our turnover rate was less than two percent annually and some of the two percent was due to retirement.

Summary

There is a certain amount of labor flexibility inherent in any operation that is not working three full shifts, seven days a week; however, real labor flexibility can only come from a well cross-trained workforce. The closer a factory moves toward flow manufacturing, the more important labor flexibility becomes. To react to Customer demand, the available labor will have to be able to perform the tasks required in filling the current orders, no matter what they are. Customer orders will rarely arrive in the mix that exactly complements the skill sets of your available labor, unless there is enough flexibility built into your labor force to meet almost any possible combination of demands as they arrive.

There are many ways to encourage your employees to learn the various skills they will need in your new Millennium Company. Reward for skills learned: Rather than paying a person for the skill level they are currently performing at and locking them into one task or set of skills, you pay them for all the skills they have mastered. This gives you the option of using them where their skills are most needed at any given moment, thereby creating greater flexibility for your organization. Also, give recognition for achievement, along with promoting the understanding that training is a valuable benefit, an investment the Company is making in your employees personally, that enhances their value to the Company and the overall job market.

A full time trainer will be a valuable asset in training your workforce. However, your factory Managers and front line Supervisors should be the folks responsible to see that cross training takes place effectively. After all, your factory Managers are the chief benefactors of a well-executed cross-training program.

CHAPTER 15

Andon Lights

One exceptional tool worth spending some time on here is the Andon light. Andon lights are devices that indicate and signal the status of a process or product. They can be simple lights, similar to traffic lights, with green lights signaling that a process is running well, yellow lights signaling a potential problem or caution, and red lights signaling a process that is stopped. They can take as many forms and applications as one's imagination can conjure up. One of the most effective and my favorite is the dot matrix display with a display area four or five inches high by about 30 inches long, capable of displaying characters and letters in a continuous scrolling manner to deliver product status messages.

These displays can be used to disseminate information about your products throughout your company, giving everyone up to the minute product status reports. The objective is to display your products' names or identification numbers in green, yellow or red. Green would signal no problems manufacturing this product. Yellow would indicate a potential problem exists for manufacturing this product within the next week or any time period you choose. This could be a potential part shortage that may or may not be resolved by the end of the chosen period. Red would indicate that you cannot manufacture this product now and you have a Customer Order that needs filling. This could be a result of an Engineering quality hold affecting the product until a technical problem is resolved or the shortage of a particular part, preventing completion of the product, etc. These product names would be continually scrolling in the color representing their status.

The Andon lights would be displayed throughout your organization. There would be a display in plain view in your Sourcing Department to ensure that your Sourcing folks know of any problems they should be working on, such as parts shortages. Engineering should have a display in their area to ensure they know about problems they can help with. Customer Service and other Supply Chain personnel should have viewing access so that they don't promise product to Customers for immediate delivery that is on hold and not available. Quality folks should be aware of any product that is on hold or has the potential of being placed on hold. Make sure you cover the common areas such as the cafeteria and hallways and on and on, throughout your entire business.

Your Shop Floor Supervisors should control the Andon lights. In a medical equipment manufacturing or other highly regulated business, you may want to have your Shop Floor Supervisor confer with your Quality Assurance or Regulatory group prior to placing a product on hold. In these types of regulated businesses, product holds can take on a life of their own. They can come under the scrutiny of various regulatory agencies at a later date, so you want to be sure that you are doing the right thing by placing the product on hold.

One reason that Andon lights are so effective is that they call a great deal of attention to an existing problem. When the Boss asks why such and such a product is on status red, you want to not only have the answer, but you want to be able to assure him that the problem is being resolved. The lights create the pressure necessary to bring focus toward resolving production problems in a timely manner. One memorable event, that stands out from my

Andon Lights

past, took place one afternoon shortly after I had taken over a factory running in the '70s mode. My Facilities Manager told me that he could not repair a sealing machine that was needed on the Production Floor because his men were tied up moving a Vice President into a new office. That was the first, last, and only time he made that mistake. Shortly after this unfortunate incident, the new Andon lights were installed. The lights help sort out and bring attention to what is really important in your business. Had the lights been up and running the day my Facilities Manager had to choose between moving the office and fixing the sealing machine, he would have had no problem understanding where the priority was.

Another important application of the Andon light is to signal personnel in your Shipping or Distribution group that an item should not be shipped. Usually the lights would be used as a fall back to whatever method is in place to ensure that product on hold is not shipped until the hold is removed. The rule can be as simple as: never ship an item that is coded red. If you intend to use your Andon light signaling system in this manner, it is important to include the Quality Assurance and or Regulatory Affairs professionals in the decision-making process. An official hold notice can be issued in the usual manner, with a copy to the individual who is responsible for changing the Andon light signaling codes. The code would then be changed to red for the affected product. Of course, when the product is removed from hold, the responsible individual will have to be notified to change the signaling code back to green.

Caution: do not use the light signaling system to disseminate insignificant information, such as upcoming minor events or holiday greetings. To maintain the integrity of the system at a high level it is important that its serious nature never be compromised. Resist all pressure from any source to use the Andon lights for frivolous items, so that it continues to command the respect that its intended purpose requires. Everyone must understand that the data transmitted is important and relevant to the success of your operation. All messages are serious and not to be taken lightly.

Another form of Andon light can be used to indicate equipment or departmental status. Equipment status lights can be simply green, yellow and red, or even more simply, green and red, green indicating no problem with the equipment and red indicating an equipment failure. If yellow is used, it can indicate equipment shutdown for maintenance or set up. Department status lights can be used to convey a manufacturing cell's current operational situation. Green could indicate all is going OK. Yellow could indicate labor or parts shortage with the ability to still do partial builds. Red could indicate a complete department shutdown.

By communicating with lights in the above manner, you are sending the right message to your employees. The message is one of open and honest communication. Your employees learn that it is good for everyone in the business to understand where the problems are. They learn that it is a good thing to expose problems so that they can be addressed and fixed in a timely fashion. There are no hidden agendas in this type of factory. No one is about to shoot the messenger. After all, the messenger is the Andon light.

Summary

Andon lights are devices that indicate and signal the status of a process or product. They can be simple lights similar to traffic lights, with green lights signaling that a process is running well, yellow lights signaling a potential problem or caution, and red lights signaling a process that is stopped. These displays can be used to disseminate information about your products throughout your company, giving everyone up to the minute product status reports. The lights create the pressure necessary to bring focus toward resolving production problems in a timely manner.

CHAPTER 16

e-business

The Internet can be an enormously effective tool for increasing productivity in your business. An Internet site is a must for the distribution of general information about your business. Informing the public through the Internet about your company and its products is commonplace today. Most companies have job opportunities posted on their web sites that are intended to attract new employees. This helps avoid paying the job placement fees charged by placement firms for job searches. Product information can be elaborate, taking potential Customers on a virtual tour of your e-showroom. Keyword hooks can be placed to attract searches to your site and agreements can be made with other related sites to attract potential Customers. There are many other practical uses for your web site, such as posting facility locations with travel directions for each location.

Many companies have taken product information to the next stage, allowing Customers to place product orders over the net. Customers can order simple products straight out or configure complex products online. In the latter instance, this can save your Sales staff many hours of face time with your Customers, working out order details. Say for instance, the sale was for a complex product with many different options and some of the options were not available on certain models, the automated ordering system could be programmed to avoid any ordering errors matching features with models that a Salesman might make. Customers are even willing to work out delivery and installation times based on an availability schedule posted and automatically updated on the net. Many companies have found that their Customers actually prefer to do their own ordering over the net, especially for more complex products, even though they are fulfilling the role normally filled by the Salesman. They can build their own product at their leisure without the pressure of a Salesman's pitch. Customers who use your products and the supplies or disposables that go with them find it convenient to order the supplies themselves. This is especially true when they know exactly what they want and are ordering the same items over and over on a regular basis.

Service is another area that clearly can benefit from the Internet. Ordering service parts and scheduling service calls are a win for both the Customer and the company. Service parts availability can be an issue with older product. Detailed parts lists can be easily posted and updated on the net. Service manuals posted on the net can reflect the latest changes and parts substitutions, making it easy for the Customer to figure out exactly what they need. Also, cross-reference sheets cross referencing your part numbers with your competition's part numbers are easy to maintain on the net.

Another fascinating use of the Internet as a tool is its application in diagnostics. A Customer can dial up a manufacturer, hook up a problem piece of equipment, then diagnose and fix the problem live in minutes. This can work with your Customers or your field service Team. The service can be offered with new products to attract new business or it can be sold with a service contract on its own, generating another form of revenue. Large equipment manufacturers are marketing this service as another source of revenue, charging a fee for improving their Customer's efficiency either by cutting power consumption or fuel consumption. The equipment can be monitored 24 hours a day and adjustments can be made while the equipment is running. Imagine being able to collect a fee for saving your Customer tens of millions of dollars a year in fuel costs by monitoring and tweaking equipment you build and supply. Just being able to determine when a Customer's piece of equipment needs to be serviced to keep it performing at an optimum level can bring a fortune in revenue.

Supply Chain Management is the area where we find the greatest use of the net in running the factory. Many suppliers offer technical assistance over the net. This is very important when designing new products. Engineers can access a vendor's database to determine the most effective electronic component to use in a circuit. The component's functional characteristics, as well as its footprint, can be quickly ascertained by using the supplier's database. Some design systems can incorporate this data, automatically preventing design errors from occurring. One nice feature about these vendor sites is that many of them are available 24 hours a day, seven days a week. An Engineer working on a design at 9:00 pm in the evening does not have to wait until 8:00 am the next day to sort out his technical issues.

Communication of your requirements to your supplier can be done automatically over the net. Rather than your sending your suppliers reams of paper updating them on the latest changes to your requirements, the suppliers can access the data themselves. This will ensure that your suppliers always have the latest up to the minute changes and can incorporate those changes into their planning. In very sophisticated relationships, a vendor may even allow your requirements to drive their requirement planning systems. If you are still working with Purchase Orders, access to your requirements online can eliminate the need to generate thousands of Purchase Order change notices. This also makes it easy to reconcile your Purchase Orders with your supplier's open orders. How many times have you been burned because you thought you had an open order your supplier thought was closed? If you are using letters of intent instead of Purchase Orders, your suppliers will be able to access the site for your latest requirements and their delivery history for the "letter of intent."

For close relationships represented by replenishment techniques such as the in-house stores, "Bread Man routine" and the Wand-to-order system, you can use the net to signal your supplier to deliver. Also, inventory transactions moving material into your stock and at the same time removing it from your vendor's stock can make life easy for you and your vendor. To carry this one step further, the transaction can set up your Accounts Payable and your vendor's Accounts Receivable at the time. Even further, funds can be transferred at the correct time, based on an agreed payment schedule. These things can only be accomplished when you are partnering with your vendors and have a good solid relationship developed with them. You can even use the net to have a vendor ship third party items (items you sell to your Customers, but a third party builds and, in this case, also ships to your Customer) directly to your Customer.

Signaling quality alerts is another effective use of the net. An alert of a potential quality problem can be sent automatically over the net, as we did earlier to solve some of our first-pass yield problems. Select members of the first-pass yield Team were sent a message when a set of predetermined criteria failed to be met. Such a system could be used to notify any number of employees whenever any measurable limit is achieved. Also, product holds can be communicated quickly to distribution personnel as well as order Management folks.

The net can be used to effectively reduce purchase cost by reducing the prices paid for material, especially when buying commodity items. The e-auction is used to heighten competition between suppliers by creating a forum that encourages your suppliers to give you the lowest price they can for the products you want to buy. An e-auction (which is really a reverse auction – it is *e-business*

your suppliers who are bidding for your business) can be created with the following characteristics:

- Your potential suppliers are invited to participate in the e-auction.
- You supply specifications, requirements and ground rules prior to the e-auction for the participating supplier's review.
- All participating suppliers sign onto the same site at the date and time of the e-auction.
- The Suppliers make their initial bids for each item they are interested in supplying your company.
- All participating suppliers can see the bids submitted by all those bidding.
- For a set period of time, say 30 minutes, the suppliers bid against each other while you watch the prices fall.
- If there are no bids during the last three minutes or so of the auction, the auction ends.
- If there is a bid in the last three minutes of the auction, the auction is extended by five minutes.
- You may or may not award the business to the lowest bidder.

My advice is to be very careful with this tool. Switching suppliers too often can adversely affect your flow manufacturing operation's effectiveness. e-auctions have their place in securing the lowest prices, but be careful not to abuse them.

Other uses of the net, either Internet or Intranet:

- Basic communication such as e-mail, meeting scheduling and confirmation.
- Meetings: there are very effective services and software packages that facilitate meetings using the net.

- Managing travel: Shopping for the best price, booking trips and confirming reservations. Most of the work is completed online by the travelers themselves, saving on personnel in the Travel Department.
- Employee evaluations, including 360-degree reviews and annual appraisals with the necessary signoffs, fit well into the e-business mix.
- Employee expenses can be submitted and approved on the net.
- Employee news can be transmitted through online employee newsletters.
- Open job positions can be posted for both internal candidates and through search firms for external searches. Other online search sites can be mined for job applicants.
- Project Management can be effectively managed for internal and external participants.
- Product changes can be approved with an online signoff procedure.

These are only a few of the many uses you will have for the Internet and Intranet in helping to manage your new Millennium business. Virtually the only limitations are those imposed by the limits of your imagination.

Summary

The net is a powerful tool that can be used to increase productivity in your business. It can be used to communicate information that will help sell your products to your Customers or allow your Customers to order their own product. The net can be used to help manage your service business. It is an excellent diagnostic tool that can be used to monitor and repair Customer equipment online.

e-business

Supply Chain Management is the area where we find the greatest use of the net in running the factory. Some of the Supply Chain uses are: technical assistance, communicating requirements to suppliers, signaling suppliers to deliver material, and managing inventory transactions, including creating the Accounts Payable transaction for you and the Accounts Receivable transaction for your supplier, as well as making the actual payment when the time comes. The e-auction is also an effective tool for lowering purchase costs.

There are many other uses for the net in conducting the day-to-day operations of a business. The possibilities are virtually endless.

PART 3
QUALITY

CHAPTER 17

Quality and First-Pass Yield

When it comes to quality, First-Pass Yield is your first line of defense. This is where you will identify not only your internal quality issues, but also your vendor's quality issues. First, let's define what we mean when we say "First-Pass Yield." This is the number of units that make it through your final test station without incident – usually expressed as a percent. In other words, of 100 units submitted for final test, 99 units pass and one unit fails. This is a First-Pass Yield of 99 percent. Any unit that gets to the end of the line and requires rework of any kind is a failure. Each failure should be recorded and the failure mode defined for further analysis, such as a Pareto analysis of all failures. This will facilitate identification of the most critical areas that are causing the failures and the ones needing attention first. Obviously, First-Pass Yields should be measured after final product burn in, if there is one, so that failures after burn in will be included in the analysis and resolution process.

The Integrity of the System

It is important to maintain the integrity of this number. It is very important that First-Pass Yield be based on the final test of the item you are building. No tweaking is acceptable. An item requiring tweaking is a failure and should be counted as such.

Tweaking is a form of waste and should be eliminated. If the reason for the tweaking is not measured, the problem (the reason for the tweaking) will not be analyzed and will never be addressed or eliminated. If you are only testing a sample of your product, then use that sample to extrapolate your First-Pass Yield. If you are not testing your product at the end of the line, you will have to move back further in the production process to a point where failures are detected. If you have no failures in your manufacturing process, you can forget this section on First-Pass Yield. After final test, the item should be ready to ship to the Customer with no further work required.

While consulting for a company, I stumbled on a perfect example of how not to measure First-Pass Yield. At one point in the Company's past, Operations Management was focusing heavily on yields. Shop Floor Management decided to install all circuit boards in a dummy production unit designated as a test bed, prior to installing the boards in the final product. Any failures would be detected prior to entering the final assembly cell. This culling process was pure waste. Its sole purpose was to make the numbers look good and even at that the First-Pass Yield numbers were only running around 80 percent. This was a case of the measurement system driving poor business practices. The circuit boards went through a final test on a very sophisticated in-circuit tester prior to being delivered to the final assembly cell. This is where the board failures should have been caught, not in the final assembly cell. If the problems had been analyzed and addressed properly, the First-Pass Yield for this product could have and would have exceeded 99 percent, as evidenced by the high yields achieved for similar products being built in a sister factory.

A world-class company will have a First-Pass Yield that exceeds 99 percent. This yield will reflect the cumulative yield of all the parts and assemblies that go into the final product at the final assembly level. With (mistake proofing) processes and Six Sigma methodology, end of the line failures can be brought down to a few parts per million. But to achieve these kinds of results, the measurement system must be one of integrity with robust processes.

The Importance of First-Pass Yield

Why is it so important to have an exceptional end of the line yield? First, product cycle time is greatly affected by end of the line yield. A complicated product like a fetal heart monitor can require over an hour and sometimes much more of final testing to demonstrate that the product is functioning correctly when it leaves the facility. In many cases the type of final testing is dictated by the requirements of the end user or a regulatory body such as the Food and Drug Administration. A failure at the end of the production line means another unit has to be built and configured in its place to fill the Customer Order while the defective unit is going through a trouble-shooting process. This process usually requires an expensive talent such as a technician to find the problem and repair the unit. In the case of medical electronics, if the unit is opened for any reason, the unit must go through all of the safety testing steps again. Not all products are regulated products; however, the effect is similar; rework is costly and causes Customer delivery delays. The second reason yield is so important is its effect on inventory. The closer to the end of the production line, the more valuable the inventory. This is the stage where the product has all the parts and subassembly present, along with all the labor that has gone into the product to get it to this stage in the manufacturing process. When these "close to finished" units are hanging around in inventory awaiting repair, they are just sucking up inventory dollars that cannot be passed on to the next asset class – Accounts Receivable and eventually cash. A third reason is overall quality. If you are experiencing high failure rates at the end of your line, chances are your Customers are also experiencing a higher than necessary Out-of-Box Failure rate. Out-of-Box Failures are failures that your Customers experience when they remove your product from its container and go to use it – plug it in. This same logic also applies to your warranty repair costs or expenses. Higher failure rates at the end of the manufacturing line will most likely translate into higher overall warranty expense for your company. All these quality issues are closely tied together.

Keep the Program Simple

If you keep the program simple, your Shop Floor production workers will manage the program for you on a day-to-day basis. Stick to easy to understand formulas, such as the one used above. Avoid creating many exceptions to the rules. Try to treat all end items in like fashion as much as is practically possible. This may not be possible in an organization where you are making very different products, such as in a medical equipment company that manufactures disposables in the same factory, which manufactures the products that use them. Avoid any attempt to just make the numbers look good by violating the spirit of the system, as in the example above where circuit boards were being culled. Make sure the operators are in charge of collecting the data, not the Quality Group. The Quality folks should be involved in the overall process, but the process owners are the production folks. Shop Floor workers should be a key part of the Team driving the process.

The Role of the Cross-Functional Self-Directed Team

A Cross-Functional Self-Directed Team is highly recommended for the purposes of driving the project during its initial stages. The initial stages will last until the First-Pass yield exceeds 99 percent. When the 99 percent is achieved, the Team should be disbanded. At this stage the Team should have in place processes that will maintain high quality levels. The Team's job is not complete until the infrastructure has been created to ensure that quality levels remain above the 99 percent level and continued

Quality and First-Pass Yield

progress toward the total elimination of all failures is also ensured. The members of the Team should be drawn from the various areas of the business that can contribute to improving First-Pass Yield. A typical Team could include representation from: Production Management, Shop Floor workers, Quality Assurance/Regulatory Affairs, Engineering, Manufacturing Engineering, and Sourcing. The Team Leader should hold regularly scheduled meetings and report the Team's progress to top Management frequently. There will be much more about Cross-Functional Self-Directed Teams in a later Chapter of this book.

This can be one of the toughest challenges in any operation. The trip from 42 percent First-Pass Yield to better than 99 percent took almost three years in one $100,000,000 plus factory I was responsible for. The Cross-Functional Self-Directed Team was the vehicle of choice to drive the project in this facility. The Team had made excellent progress initially, driving First-Pass Yield from 42 percent to around 90 percent. However, the Team was stuck at the 90 percent level for almost a year. Progress had stalled, the Team members were becoming increasingly frustrated, and Management was not happy. The Team Leader wanted to resign and an excellent Shop Floor worker wanted out of his Team member role. His reason was he felt that there was nothing more he could contribute. In frustration, I requested an invitation to speak to the Team. (Self-Directed Teams will not be Self-Directed unless you make them understand they are completely in charge of solving the challenge handed them. Hence, the request for an invitation to speak to the Team.) The Team honored my request and I was invited to the next Team meeting. I asked why they had not placed anyone on their Team from our sister factory, which was manufacturing the surface mount boards for many of the products we manufactured in our plant. They agreed to take a look at making the addition to the Team and indeed, they did add a representative from our sister factory the following week.

Second, I recommended a vendor who supplied most of the electronic components that went into the product be added to the Team, as it appeared that "random component failures" were causing a significant number of the end of the line failures. This suggestion, too, was taken to heart and a key vendor was brought in to consult. Lastly, I addressed the issue of the Team Leader and the Shop Floor worker wanting to resign. I pointed out that most of these issues were related to the job of the Facilitator and asked who the Team Facilitator was. I truly could not recall. I was told that the Production Manager was the Facilitator. My reaction was, "That's no good. The Production Manager has too much to gain or lose from the success of every meeting. He will be too focused and intimate with the problems being addressed to keep his eye on how the Team process is functioning. The Facilitator must be someone a little more removed from the day-to-day happenings on the Shop Floor. A little detachment from the technical issues affecting First-Pass Yield will allow him or her to sit back and take in the interaction of the Team members. How is the Production Manager going to watch the overall process to ensure things like Team member participation?" I asked my Manufacturing Manager how he got to be the Team Facilitator and he told me I appointed him. After a little embarrassment and a few laughs, all at my expense, I suggested that we tap the talents of our Human Resource Manager for the slot of Team Facilitator. This suggestion also was well received and the Human Resource Manager agreed to take the job. Within six months First-Pass Yield exceeded 99 percent.

First-Pass Yield Quality Alerts

More than three failures of the same type in any manufacturing cell in any given day should trigger an alert to key Team members. The more automatic you can make the alert being sent out, the better. If automated test equipment is involved, chances are there is a PC somewhere in the loop or one can be added. The

Quality and First-Pass Yield

PC can be networked and programmed to trigger the sending of a message to key Team members when a given target is hit, such as three failures on the same day. The limit should be one that makes sense for your business. Also, if there is a business or ERP system that is present on the Shop Floor, this system can be utilized to send and deliver the triggered message to the relevant Team members. To carry this process one step further, a signal warning of the failures can be routed to pagers or cell phones being worn by the key Team members. However, the message can be a simple phone call to the Team members from the production cell with the problem or Andon lights can be used to deliver the message. The point is to involve the Team at the point in time when the problem is occurring, rather than have the Team just reviewing the problem after the fact. There is no substitute for observing the actual product experiencing the problem when the problem is taking place. The product can be placed on hold, preventing further rejects from being created, until the problem is temporarily or permanently resolved. The next step is to do the root cause analysis that will identify the real cause of the problem and lead to a mistake-proofed solution.

Quality Related Tracking and Identification

To have an effective First-Pass Yield improvement program, a company must be able to identify, track and categorize the causes of its end of the line failures. The tracking ability should drill down to the lowest component level in the product's bill-of-material. For instance, component failures should be traceable to each component on the circuit boards that are part of the upper level assembly. This information will be necessary to identify fixes that will improve designs by eliminating repeat offenders, such as replacing a component that fails too often with a more robust component that will avoid the failure mode in the future. It will also be necessary to identify failure conditions at the component level that could be workmanship related or random component failures from the original manufacture level.

An automated data collection system is a convenient way to collect data, but it is not absolutely necessary. Several types of test equipment will identify and categorize the types of failures that occur. The in-circuit tester is one. Also, with the utilization of a data collection system, the type of failure problem encountered can be scanned from a menu of common failures with bar codes placed next to the failure mode. This has the advantage of categorizing most failures when they are being scanned, with the exception of the failures that do not fit any of the predefined causes; these would be scanned into the "other category" and defined by keyboard entry. The downside here is that it is easy for an operator to select an inaccurate failure mode from the bar code menu and record the failure incorrectly. In the absence of an automated system, simply documenting each failure for further analysis, either directly into a database on a PC located in the manufacturing cell or on a hand-written log for later analysis, is all that is necessary. The size and nature of the manufacturing operation will dictate which method of recording failures makes sense. Remember it is not necessary to spend large sums of money implementing sophisticated systems to move your operation in the direction of a new Millennium organization. In fact, just the opposite is true. Remember, even the MRP or ERP system takes on a lesser degree of importance in the factory as the operation becomes more dependent on Kanban signals and flow-manufacturing techniques for inventory replenishment.

Summarizing, Categorizing and Analyzing the Data

Once the failure data has been collected, it must be summarized, categorized and analyzed. To be useful, the data should be presented so that repeat offenders and trends are easily recognizable. A simple analysis can point to the failure modes that yield the biggest payoff when the problem is solved. This is the fuel

Quality and First-Pass Yield

that the First-Pass Yield Team will use to attack the failure issues. Since the Team is Cross-Functional, all the talent necessary to address the issues uncovered should be part of the Team; if not, the Team should have the clout necessary to acquire any additional talent it may need to address the failure issues. Adding vendors to the Team mix makes for an even more powerful problem-busting group. Six Sigma methodologies can be a powerful tool in getting to root causes and finding failure solutions. Break the issues down into the following four categories: high payoff, low difficulty; low payoff, low difficulty; high payoff, high difficulty; low payoff, high difficulty. The first problems to go after and solve should be the low hanging fruit that falls into the category of big payoff, easy to fix. Next go after the items with low difficulty and low payoff. The reasoning here is that these low difficulty issues can be quickly fixed, demonstrating the success of the program. Even though the payoff is low, the support that the successes will win merits the low difficulty, low payoff items the number two slot on the priority list. Next, go after the failures with a high payoff and a high difficulty level. Lastly, tackle the items with low payoff and a high level of difficulty. Under some circumstances these items are and should be forgotten, but not when it comes to First-Pass Yield. Here, we need to wring every bit of opportunity out of fixing every problem we identify. Remember we are after very lofty results. If you have five major subassemblies that go into an upper level assembly and the yield on each of the five subassemblies are at the 99 percent level, you will be hard pressed to achieve yields greater than 95 percent. The simple math looks like this: $.99 \times .99 \times .99 \times .99 \times .99 = .95099$.

Implementing the Corrective Action

The Team should be actively making engineering change recommendations. Many of the problems will find their resolution in the Engineering or Manufacturing Engineering arenas. Even if the designs are not the cause of the problems, very often an engineering change can ensure that the problem does not reoccur. This may just take the form of reviewing a recommended change and then documenting that change. In the case of a regulated business such as a medical equipment manufacturer, just about every significant change must be evaluated to determine its overall effects on the product's efficacy. And still more complicated changes require clinical testing before a change can be implemented. Budgetary constraints will inevitably lead to resistance on projects that require a great deal of engineering resources. Nevertheless, the Team must be committed to resolving these issues and fixing the problems that have been surfaced. Some good old-fashioned ingenuity at creating alternative solutions will be helpful in these situations. For example: you may want to change the color of the wires that plug into a panel connector so that the colors of the wires match the color on the connectors to correct miswiring problem. However, Engineering would have to change the service manual documentation when the colors of the wires are changed. A temporary solution not involving any Engineering time could be to tag and number the wires with the color and then remove the tags during final test. Not a perfect solution, but one that will work until the more permanent solution of changing the wire colors can be implemented.

Of course, many corrective actions do not require an Engineering change or even engineering involvement. Poka-yoke (mistake proofing) process improvements can be simple methods changes or modifications to tools, fixtures and test equipment. One example was cited earlier in the Poka-yoke solution for configuration software. The test equipment software was changed to verify the setting of the DIP switches in a medical monitoring device. The solution prevented the final test from being completed unless the switches were configured to accommodate the product configuration. Notching components to ensure proper orientation is another example. One of my favorites was used by a manufacturer of LED's and Infrared products. The current that ran the equipment was conducted through the components. If the components had a short (open), the equipment would stop because the power would stop once the component with the short reached the stage in the process where it was conducting the power to run the equipment. Violà, no more components with shorts ever reached the subassembly stage.

Do not Build in Lots

Don't build assemblies in lots, then sort out the rejects and use the good ones. This practice leaves the rejects to hang around, eating up inventory dollars with the promise of a repair someday; that is, until you throw them out and take the inventory write down. Build assemblies and subassemblies in as small a quantity as is practically possible. The goal is to build everything only in lots of one. Building in larger lots only means larger inventories and larger scrap piles. If a process does go awry in large lot building, and the defect is discovered later down the line, you will have to deal with the whole lot. If you build in lots of one only and pass the item on to the next station in the process before making the next item, you will only have one reject to deal with.

Building all assemblies in the final assembly cell and immediately passing the item on to the next station goes a long way towards solving the above problem. The manufacturing process can, in many cases, be designed so that the next stage in the assembly process can verify the quality of the components being assembled. After production areas are arranged into linked-cells, work should begin on integrating all the subassemblies into the final assembly cell. This can be done over time, gradually pulling in one assembly after another. One actual example that took several months to integrate into one cell is as follows: First, the manufacturing cell was created around the upper level assembly, then the printer assembly was added to one bench in the cell. Next the cable assemblies were built in the same cell one at a time as they were needed, at the stage they were used in the upper level assembly process. Getting away from building in lots will improve your First-Pass Yield because you will never have piles of rejects created in lots and undiscovered until they show up in the final assembly process or the final test of the product. There were some items, such as circuit boards, which went into the upper level assembly that did not make sense to manufacture in the final assembly cell. In these cases, let common sense be the guide in deciding what assemblies to bring into the final assembly cell.

SPC Statistical Process Control

Statistical Process Control (SPC) can be a major contributor in improving a product's First-Pass Yield. SPC puts the Shop Floor operators in charge of the manufacturing process. This will eliminate the need for Quality Control Inspectors, freeing up these people for more productive activities. All inspection is waste. In some highly regulated businesses it may not be possible to eliminate all inspection, in order to comply with Government regulations. However, even the Government is becoming enlightened and is willing to accept the elimination of inspection, provided it can be demonstrated that a high level of quality can be maintained. Eliminating inspectors eliminates conflict in the workplace. Imagine a scenario where your processes are not capable of making a good item on a repeatable basis, then add to this an Inspector who inspects someone else's work which is affected by these out of control processes. The Inspector rejects your best effort's hard work. This breeds a natural environment for conflict. Not an atmosphere most people could be happy working in, yet there are thousands of factories out there in manufacturing land USA that exhibit these characteristics. Using SPC to monitor the manufacturing processes can eliminate the need for Inspectors, greatly improving your quality and making your factory a much more pleasant and friendly place to work. We will explore SPC in more detail in a later Chapter in this book.

Poka-yoke: Mistake Proofing Your Processes

Mistake proofing your processes, or creating conditions in your manufacturing processes that ensure mistakes cannot happen, can be a major contributor to a successful First-Pass Yield improvement program. This effort should begin with some formal training. Either hire a firm that specializes in this type of training or pick an individual who will be your trainer for this topic and have that individual trained. A combination of getting outside help and training your own trainer can get the training rolling quickly. Train everyone who is connected with the design or manufacture of the product. Just one or two days of classes can be very effective. The training is as much about awareness as it is about the specific knowledge that will be passed.

Making it impossible for your employees to make mistakes is not as complicated as it sounds. It is also one of the most creative and fun projects your people will get a chance to be involved with. The satisfaction of coming up with a solution to a problem which eliminates that problem forever is intense and contagious. A degree in Engineering is not necessary, and as we are looking for simple solutions, this may even give the amateur an edge. Everyone can draw on his or her everyday life experiences to find examples of mistake proofing. Some examples follow:

- Keys cannot be removed from a car's ignition unless the shift lever is in park.
- Auto Gas tank fill pipes will not allow diesel fuel pump nozzles to be inserted, preventing the driver from accidentally putting diesel fuel in a gas tank.
- Dead man switches on trains and lawn mowers: When the handle is released the train or lawn mower automatically stops.
- Sensors on sinks that start when the presence of your hand is detected and stop when your hand is removed.

There are many other examples that everyone can come up with from his or her own experiences. The point is that we all have had exposure to this type of technology and can contribute in finding mistake-proofing solutions. The folks that will contribute the most to this effort are the folks that handle the day-to-day activity, the Shop Floor workers in the factory atmosphere. Make sure to involve them in the mistake proofing effort.

Six Sigma

Both Statistical Process Control (SPC) and mistake proofing (Poka-yoke) are Six Sigma tools. We have talked about each of these tools throughout this book. Of course, each of these tools can be used separately and do not have to be part of a Six Sigma program. Many smaller organizations will shy away from a full-blown Six Sigma program, which can be expensive and difficult to implement. Six Sigma requires a much more complex infrastructure for training and larger resource commitment for support than does a Statistical Process Control program. Sure, it would be nice if the resources were available for a full-blown Six Sigma program; however, much progress can be made using the simpler tools, such as SPC. So if you are a smaller organization, start with SPC and when you collect from the payoff of your efforts here, move on to Six Sigma, but don't think for a minute that you cannot compete without it.

In fact, I want to pass on a warning here. On one of my consulting experiences, I found myself answering questions for a multibillion dollar US company that was thinking about going ahead with a Six Sigma program. When the individual started to talk about training and certification for just about every employee, I was compelled to raise a red flag. I was familiar with the type of program they were talking about. The requirements are for several days of intense training, over a two to three week period and a commitment of roughly 20% of each employee's time for project work. I was also familiar with the organization that was asking the questions. All this led me to caution that if the employees involved in the Six Sigma program just cut that time out of their regular workday rather than working extra to cover their new commitments, it could bring things at the company to a halt. The point is: know your employees and seek their commitment prior to embarking on a Six Sigma program.

All the above considered, Six Sigma is a powerful force that can move any company ahead quickly. When a company arrives at the Six Sigma quality level, they will be operating in an environment with 3.4 defects per million opportunities. This is pretty heady stuff when you consider that most companies would be happy to operate in an environment somewhere between three and four sigma, which is between 6,210 and 66,000 defects per million opportunities. By applying Six Sigma tools, you will understand and be able to control your processes. Capability studies will let you discover statistically whether your processes are capable of manufacturing a good repeatable product or not. If your processes are out of control, the Six Sigma tools will allow you to discover what needs to be corrected and the optimum methodology to employ in making the corrections.

There will be several levels of involvement from different parts of the organization. First, the success of this program will largely depend on the support that comes from top Management — the Champions. The Champions are the individuals that will give the go-ahead and talk up the program. They will clear the way through the resistance. Second, Master Black Belts, usually a full time position, will develop and provide the bulk of the training. One of the most important functions of the Master Black Belts will be to help select the projects to be worked on. It is very important that the projects selected be ones that complement the goals of the entire organization. This is the key to the success of the entire program. The organization can have the best training and the most talented staff in the business, but to what end would this be if resources were devoted to irrelevant projects?

Third, the Black Belts are assigned to an area of the business such as manufacturing where they usually work full time on key projects. They also assist the Master Black Belts with training and assist their students with their projects. Fourth, Green Belts make up the bulk of the Six Sigma Team and are working on projects in the normal course of their regular jobs. They seek opportunities for improvement in the areas where they normally work and apply their Six Sigma skills to improve every area of the business. Together, these four groups make up the Six Sigma Team that will drive the entire organization to serve the Customer by delivering a higher quality product or service at a lower cost when the Customer wants it.

Project selection is where the opportunities are identified. Once the employees are trained, the organization will want a return on its investment. Only through judicious project selection can the Company profit from its investment. The problem to be solved should lend itself to Six Sigma methodology; this demands that the problem be defined in such a way that it is clearly understood. The affecting factors must be measurable in a meaningful way. Analyzing the data should lead to clearly identifying the root causes. The process should lend itself to finding the best solution and the controls that when put in place ensure that the problem does not reoccur. Don't try to boil the ocean. Keep the projects manageable in size. And again, no "make work" projects here. Only projects that contribute directly to achieving the organization's goals should be considered.

Six Sigma can be applied to just about any area of your business, not just manufacturing. It works well in Engineering in its application to new product design. Back office activities such as Order Management, Finance and Accounting, Collections and Payables, e-business and Quality can be improved through the elimination or automation of routine tasks. Marketing and Sales organizations will find the Six Sigma programs which involve the Customer and the Customer's organization a powerful selling

Quality and First-Pass Yield

tool. Service organizations will use these tools to enhance Customer service, accurately predict the Customer's service requirements and maximize profit.

What is in it for your people? Not just the fun – and it is fun, albeit a lot of hard work. It is an investment in your employees. The new skills are in high demand and will make your employees more marketable. Six Sigma will contribute not only to the organization's growth, it will also contribute to your employees' personal and professional growth. These tools can be applied to virtually all facets of one's life. Everybody wants to be the best and work for the best: these skills definitely make one a cut above the pack. The availability of this type of training will definitely attract the best job applicants. One of the most attractive benefits your employees will reap from the program is the elimination of politics in project selection decisions. If someone has had a worthy project that has been blocked for political reasons, Six Sigma applied correctly will surface that project and slot it for execution. The nature of the process dictates that the numbers and the logic will determine which projects are selected for pursuit.

Following is a list of some of the Six Sigma tools. This will give those unfamiliar with the process an idea of the nature and scope of the Six Sigma toolbox.

- Benchmarking
- Brainstorming
- Control charts
- Capability analysis
- Histogram – frequency distribution
- Pareto – sorting the important few from the many
- QFD – Quality Function Deployment
- FMEA – Failure Mode and Effects Analysis
- Gage R&R – Gage repeatability and reproducibility

- Process mapping
- DOE – Design of Experiments
- C & E – Cause and Effect Analysis

And finally, a couple of thoughts to ponder:

"Statistical thinking will one day be as necessary for efficient citizenship as the ability to read and write." — H.G. Wells

"The problems that exist in the world today...cannot be solved by the level of thinking that created them." —Albert Einstein

Summary

First-Pass Yield is your first line of defense in your quest for superior quality. This is where you will identify not only your internal quality issues, but also you vendor's quality issues. First-Pass Yield is the number of units that make it through your final test station without incident – usually expressed as a percent. In other words, of 100 units submitted for final test, 99 units pass and one unit fails. This is a First-Pass Yield of 99 percent. Each failure should be recorded and the failure mode defined for further analysis and identification of the areas that are causing the failures.

Here are three reasons why it is important to have an exceptional end of the line yield. First, product cycle time is greatly affected by the end of the line yield. Rework is costly and causes Customer delivery delays. Second, First-Pass Yield's effect on inventory is very significant. The closer to the end of the production line, the more valuable the inventory. When these "close to finished" units are hanging around in inventory awaiting repair, they are just sucking up inventory dollars that cannot be passed on to the next asset class – Accounts Receivable and eventually cash. Third is First-Pass Yield's effect on overall quality. If you are experiencing high failure rates at the end of your line, chances are your Customers are also experiencing a higher than

Quality and First-Pass Yield

necessary Out-of-Box Failure rate. This same logic also applies to your warranty repair costs or expenses. Higher failure rates at the end of the manufacturing line will most likely translate into higher overall warranty expense for your Company. All these quality issues are closely tied together.

To have an effective First-Pass Yield improvement program, a Company must be able to identify, track and categorize the causes of its end of the line failures. The tracking ability should drill down to the lowest component level in the product's bill-of-material. This information will be necessary to identify fixes that will improve designs by eliminating repeat offenders. It will also be necessary to identify failure conditions at the component level that could be workmanship related or random component failures from the original manufacture level.

Many of the problems will find their resolution in the Engineering or Manufacturing Engineering arenas. Many corrective actions do not require an Engineering change or even Engineering involvement. Poka-yoke (mistake proofing) process improvements can be simple method changes or modifications to tools, fixtures and test equipment.

Statistical Process Control () can be a major contributor in improving a product's First-Pass Yield. SPC puts the Shop Floor operators in charge of the Manufacturing process. Also, mistake proofing your processes or creating conditions in your manufacturing processes that ensure mistakes cannot happen can be a major contributor to a successful First-Pass Yield improvement program. Both Statistical Process Control (SPC) and mistake proofing (Poka-yoke) are Six Sigma tools. Six Sigma is a powerful force that can move any Company ahead quickly. When a company arrives at the Six Sigma quality level, they will be operating in an environment with 3.4 defects per million opportunities. If someone has had a worthy project that has been blocked for political reasons, Six Sigma applied correctly will surface that project and slot it for execution. The nature of the process dictates that the numbers and the logic will determine which projects are selected for pursuit.

CHAPTER 18

Quality and Statistical Process Control

As previously discussed, Statistical Process Control (SPC) is far less complicated and less expensive to implement than Six Sigma. For the smaller company, SPC could be the solution of choice to begin moving on the quality path toward a new Millennium manufacturing company. When growth and funding permit, a more expansive approach can be taken and the organization can gravitate toward Six Sigma. You will lose no time by focusing on Statistical Process Control; it is a powerful part of the Six Sigma family. For these reasons and the benefits that can be derived from SPC, I will spend quite a bit of time expanding on the subject here.

The program will wrestle responsibility for quality, problem identification, problem solving, and process/product improvement from Management and redistribute the responsibility to all the employees involved with the manufacturing process. So powerful is the process that through Team involvement the spirit of continuous improvement can spill over into virtually every area of the Company.

When I took over one of my factories, I found a very unhappy workforce. In addition to losing money, this Union factory had 30 Shop Floor inspectors for 120 Shop Floor workers. The processes were out of control, preventing the operators from making a good product, no matter how badly they wanted to. The Union grievances were many. The animosity between inspectors who delighted in finding and reporting failures and the production workers who were desperately trying to build a quality product was intense. The implementation of SPC was instrumental in turning this operation around. And SPC more than anything gets the credit for changing the work environment to a congenial, friendly place to work. Process capability studies were conducted, the processes not capable of manufacturing a quality item on a repeatable basis were identified, and the processes were fixed. The 30 Shop Floor Inspectors, who were no longer needed, were given more productive work to do. Some elected to leave – to move on and torture other employees in other companies where they would continue to work as inspectors. But in my factory, SPC and the Shop Floor workers themselves were now in charge of quality, and all 30 inspectors were gone. The quality of the products produced in this factory skyrocketed and remained at their lofty levels for years to come. Spirits also climbed along with the improvement in quality.

Statistical Process Control can be defined as a method of monitoring the production process to detect the probability of defects occurring in that process. When the probability of a defect occurring is detected through statistical analysis, the process can be halted and brought under control to prevent the defect. The emphasis is on controlling the process and preventing defects, rather than screening out the defects through inspection. For example, say you were cutting a tube into 1-inch pieces on a lathe. The acceptable limits were 1" + or - 20 thousands. One approach would be to set up the lathe, make 1,000 pieces and inspect them all at one time after they were all made. If the process went out of control after the first 50 pieces were made, you would have 950 rejects. Another approach is to control the process by monitoring it statistically (Statistical Process Control). The first step would be to determine if the process is capable of holding the tolerance of + or - 20 thousands for all parts manufactured. Let us assume that we have done this. Let us also assume that through statistical calculations we have determined that in order to maintain the tolerance of + or - 20 thousands for all the pieces, it is necessary for us to check every 50th piece produced to the tighter tolerance of + or – 10 thousands. Provided all parts checked during the process fall within the tighter limits, all the parts produced will fall within the + or - 20 thousands specification. If the process should go out of control, the maximum number of rejects that could result before detection and correction would be 50 pieces. This is a very simplified definition of Statistical Process Control. It is not the intention of this Chapter to create a detailed manual for the implementation of SPC, but rather to proselytize SPC for the benefits the program can bring about. It is only to give a general understanding of how Statistical Process Control (SPC) works that the definition is presented here.

In many instances the employee involvement is a powerful force that makes SPC work. The statistical portion of Statistical Process Control can often be seen as merely the vehicle used to bring about employee involvement that results in a culture change. This culture change can bring about a very successful Team approach involving Shop Floor workers, First Line Supervisors and Management in the identification and solving of manufacturing problems. The SPC transformation can take place over a relatively short period of six to nine months. In this short period of time, your employees' philosophy can be transformed from the traditional "that is not my problem" philosophy to the Statistical Process Control philosophical approach to problem solving that makes manufacturing problems and their resolutions the responsibility of all employees.

In one of my factories in the mid '80s I witnessed employees with less than a high school education, working in a Union shop, gathering together on their own time evenings to put together first-class Team presentations to be presented to the SPC Steering Committee, composed of the President and his immediate staff. These folks loved their newfound involvement. They were willing to give up their personal time to perfect their work, even though the Company certainly did not require it.

In this instance the pilot Teams alone turned in enough cost savings to pay for the entire out-of-pocket cost to implement the program. With over $150,000 of direct cost savings generated in the learning stage of the program, no one could deny its success. This hard dollar return was only a small part of the benefits derived from Statistical Process Control. Through this process the Team approach was born in this facility. Other future Teams involved in the Lean Manufacturing process were to benefit from the teaching of Statistical Process Control's problem-solving techniques and Team approach.

Another benefit from Statistical Process Control that cannot go unmentioned is the fun factor. After an initial period of anguish that so often accompanies the introduction of change, the employees will develop a new level of respect for each other, especially between Management and the Shop Floor worker. This new respect will bring about a spirit of cooperation, making all work in the facility more pleasurable.

Implementation

Unless there is an employee in your facility with enough experience, it is probably best to seek outside help in implementing SPC. Without outside assistance, the program will be difficult to get off the ground. You will need someone skilled in teaching problem-solving techniques to make the program a success. So, the obvious thing to do is to look for a consulting firm that has the expertise necessary to assist with implementing the program. There are many excellent firms available and willing to help.

Top Management Training:

Top operation Management training sessions should be held first, preferably off site. The objectives should be as follows:

- Form a Steering Committee – usually all those present become the Steering Committee. They would be the President and those who report to him or her.

- Decide on a driver for the project. The driver should be the individual that will push the program through to its successful conclusion. Here there is only one choice. Statistical Process Control should be a Manufacturing driven program, not a Quality Control driven program. Manufacturing has the most to gain from the successful implementation of SPC and, therefore, the highest vested interest. Also, the people that make this program work – the workers on the Shop Floor – report to the Manufacturing organization.

- Present a general overview of the program, how it works and the results that can be expected. Included should be a brief review of the math and statistical theory that is involved. Today there are several software packages that will deal nicely with the statistics. No one should fear the statistics.

- Give a description of the implementation process, potential pitfalls and resistance that could be expected. Up-front resistance can be expected from First-Line Supervision. Not all, but many, feel that their authority is being challenged when workers reporting to them are asked to identify and solve problems with the manufacturing process, a function traditionally left to First-Line Supervision until most recently.

- Formulate a mission statement. One example is included here:

Manufacturing Mission

Manufacturing's sole purpose for existence is to manufacture good quality products at the lowest possible cost with on-time delivery to our Customers, thereby earning an optimum profit for our investors, while perpetuating the business and providing a pleasant working environment for our employees.

Management's part is to see that all material, labor and equipment placed in our charge remains focused on the efficient pursuit of the above objective through the creation of an environment that fosters Continuous Improvement and the elimination of waste.

- Select the pilot projects. The pilot projects selected should be in areas that are easy to understand and can produce significant measurable results with high visibility in a short period of time. The results achieved in these areas will win over all the skeptics that do not support and even openly try to discredit the program. One huge advantage of this program is that it can survive and win out even with a high level of criticism.

- Do preliminary selection of the key players on the pilot Teams. Select only those you believe will be motivated to make the program a success. Remember that the pilot project can determine the success or failure of the entire program.

- Select one or two individuals to serve as project facilitators. These individuals should be sent for an intensive training course. The course will prepare them to instruct other Team members in the techniques of Statistical Process Control. They will become the teachers who will carry on the instructive work after the initial implementation process is complete. These will be full time positions. If more than one facilitator is selected, select one from the ranks of middle Management and another from the Shop Floor or Union bargaining unit, if there is a bargaining unit present in the organization. The facilitators should be individuals who are respected by their peers, smart enough to understand the concepts of Statistical Process Control, exhibit some leadership qualities and, of course, are willing to accept the responsibility of becoming facilitators.

All should emerge from the top Management training meetings with a much better understanding of their roles in the implementation process.

Middle Management and First-Line Supervision Training:

Classes should be held to introduce all middle Management and first-line Supervision to the program. Again, the instructors will probably be consultants or professional trainers, unless this talent is already present in the business. A representative from top Management should open each session with a statement of commitment and support. The balance of the meeting will be spent describing Statistical Process Control and the results that are expected to be achieved. The mission statement should be presented and top Management's position on the program should be made clear. Then the Managers and Supervisors should be asked for their support in making the program a success.

Don't be surprised if the skepticism on the part of the middle Managers and First-Line Supervisors is far greater than all the other groups of employees put together. Some in this group may be quite vocal, making their position of disbelief in the program's ability to help solve problems widely known. Then there will be those who will give the program lip service to upper Management, but work behind the scenes to discredit the program. At first this negativism may appear to be too great to overcome, but this should not be so. This attitude on the part of some of the First-Line Supervisors is not at all unusual. These are the folks that feel most threatened by a program that bases its success on turning responsibility for identifying and resolving problems over to the Shop Floor workers. After a few successes in the Pilot Team stages of the program, even the most skeptical of this group will come around and embrace SPC. In fact, many of the most vocal opponents of the program will usually become the most ardent supporters of the use of Statistical Process Control.

Facilitator Training:

This phase of the implementation process begins with the selection of the employees who will serve as project facilitators. The facilitators, in addition to assisting with the implementation, will be taking over from the consulting group, if one is used, after the initial phase is complete.

The Facilitators prepare for their assignments by attending a Facilitator training seminar. The seminar should cover problem identification and problem-solving techniques, the technique of qualifying a process, (determining a process's capability of producing repeatable results that are the desired results), the basic math required to control the manufacturing process and the development and maintenance of control charts. Subjects also covered should be preparing presentations and teaching others how to use the skills the Facilitators have learned.

Classroom and on-the-job Training For the Pilot Teams:

The Pilot Teams should be selected from the departments participating in the pilot projects. After the individuals who are the closest to the problems are selected, the Pilot Team should receive formal classroom training. The training should include the process of continuous improvement through the use of statistical Management, using charts, graphs, a statistical calculator or statistical software, capability studies and the methods of implementing Statistical Process Control.

Quality and Statistical Process Control

The students will probably work hard. Usually when you begin to show the Shop Floor worker that he or she is important enough for the Company to make an investment in him or her, the response is to return that investment many fold. This simple principle seems to be one of the most difficult ideas to get across to some middle Managers. Factory workers usually respond so well to the attention that they become the champions of Statistical Process Control. They usually leave the classes all charged up and eager to make improvements to the manufacturing process. Their enthusiasm becomes infectious and spreads to the other Shop Floor workers who will become involved in future SPC projects.

The skills taught in the classroom will be sharpened during the on-the-job training sessions. The Team members will then have an opportunity to apply classroom theory to real, everyday problems that they encounter on the job. This is where the Facilitators will earn their keep. Constantly being called on to resolve problems, and select methods of charting and collecting statistics, the facilitators will be kept very busy. The real payoff begins when the Pilot Teams have been trained and set out to find and resolve problems on the factory floor.

Steering Committee Meetings:

This can be a sight to behold! I have witnessed Shop Floor workers, some with less than a high school education and speaking broken English, putting together a first-class presentation so that the Company's top Management Team could see the results of their efforts. It is enough to choke you up when these people get up there and thank you for having enough faith in their abilities to trust them with an important assignment like Statistical Process Control. As I have said before, I have seen Team members meet after hours, sometimes at one of the Team member's homes on their own time, to perfect their presentations, and in a Union shop.

If the Team feels they need a new talent added to the Team, they should request the assistance at this time. Usually the requests for assistance will involve assistance from Purchasing, Manufacturing Engineering or the Information Technology group. The Teams will seek and should receive feedback from the Steering Committee. The Steering Committee should do everything it can to support the Shop Floor Teams. The Steering Committee should encourage the Team and sweep away all roadblocks in the Team's path.

Oil Leaks:

One great example of a problem addressed by a final assembly Pilot Team was x-ray housing oil leaks. The x-ray producing rotating anode device was sealed in a glass envelope. This tube, as it was called, was assembled into a leaded metal housing that was then filled with oil for cooling purposes. The metal sections had o-ring grooves machined in them and the o-ring seals prevented the oil from leaking out. After the tubes were assembled, they would be tested under power. This test produced a considerable amount of heat. It was at this stage that the oil leaks were detected. These oil leak problems persisted for years despite a great deal of attention by Manufacturing Management, Engineering and Quality Control. Machined surfaces were improved, o-ring materials were changed, o-rings were soaked in oil for days prior to being used and rigid specifications were imposed, but most of the oil leaks persisted. The oil leaks persisted until the SPC Final Assembly Department Pilot Team took on the problem.

The Team reviewed the problems carefully, using the problem-solving techniques they had learned in the classroom and on the Shop Floor. Before long they had solved one of the most serious problems. The solution was so simple that for years the solution had eluded our best Engineers. In the process of assembling the metal-to-metal sections with the o-ring in between, the Operator applied petroleum jelly to the o-ring before placing it in the o-ring groove. The assembly specification did not specify how much petroleum jelly to use; therefore, some Operators used more than others. Some Operators, believing that more is better, applied gobs of petroleum jelly. When the housing was heated during test, the petroleum jelly turned to a liquid and gave the appearance of an oil leak. Since the oil used in the housing was virtually identical in appearance to petroleum jelly in a liquid state, the housing was deemed to be a "leaker" and the unit was disassembled and reworked at great expense.

The SPC Pilot Team figured out what was happening. After all, they were the people who were closest to the operation, so it follows that with the proper training and motivation they should be the people best qualified to resolve the problem. In this case, as in so many cases, the problem was not what it appeared to be; the housing was not leaking oil from inside. The solution was simply to specify a light coating of petroleum jelly. The results turned in by the Pilot Team in solving this oil leak problem and other oil leak problems amounted to an 85 percent reduction in oil leaks.

Results From the SPC Investment

In the factory above with the oil leaks problems, in less than one year from the date of the SPC top Management kickoff meeting, scrap rates were reduced by $400,000.00 on an annualized basis. In addition, product performance, as measured by improved warranty scan life, was contributing an additional $1,800,000.00 to the bottom line on an annualized basis. These are the kind of results an SPC Continuous Improvement Program can deliver.

Employee involvement and empowerment through the formation of Shop Floor Teams to resolve problems and foster an environment of continuous improvement can prove to be valuable in achieving other Company goals. Later in this book I will expand on the "Cross-Functional Self-Directed Work Team" approach.

Summary

Statistical Process Control can be defined as a method of monitoring the production process to detect the probability of defects occurring in that process. When through statistical analysis, the probability of a defect occurring is detected, the process can be halted and brought under control to prevent the defect. The emphasis is on controlling the process and preventing defects, rather than screening out the defects through inspection.

The program will wrestle responsibility for quality, problem identification, problem solving, and process/product improvement from Management and redistribute the responsibility to all the employees involved with the manufacturing process. So powerful is the process that through Team involvement the spirit of continuous improvement can spill over into virtually every area of the company.

It is probably best to seek outside help in implementing SPC. You will need someone skilled in teaching problem-solving techniques to make the program a success. Areas of training will include: top Management training, middle Management and First-Line Supervision training, Facilitator training and classroom and on-the-job training for the Pilot Teams. Your investment in implementing Statistical Process Control will be returned quickly and many fold.

CHAPTER 19

Quality and Mistake Proofing (Poka-yoke)

Mistake Proofing was perfected to an art form by the Japanese in the late 1970s and 1980s. They called it "Poka-yoke" – a close direct translation is "fool proofing." The intent is to minimize the possibility of a workmanship error through the use of warnings, or to completely eliminate workmanship errors through the "fool proofing" of processes, making work virtually error free. Mistake proofing is based primarily on simple technology that can be easily grasped by virtually anyone. By applying common sense solutions that seek to permanently fix every day problems which arise in the workplace, processes become free of errors, making expensive inspections unnecessary and eliminating costly scrap and rework. Even 100% inspection will not catch all the defects. When mistakes are made repeatedly, look to the process for the solution, not to the operator. Everyone makes mistakes and there are hundreds of reasons mistakes are made. Fatigue, boredom, distractions, poor designs, equipment problems, difficult working conditions and personal illness are just a few reasons mistakes are made. Very few, if any, workers get up and come to work in the morning with the intention of making as many mistakes as possible that day. Nobody really wants to make mistakes by definition. Once this simple premise is accepted, it makes it easy to look to the processes or designs for solutions to manufacturing problems. The design may be a good one that works well; however, maybe its manufacturability can be improved by changing the design just a little to make it easier to build. This is not to say the design is poor, but only that it can be improved. The more manufacturable a design is made, the more accepted and the more useful the design will be.

One of the most powerful characteristics of mistake proofing is that everyone in your facility can participate. All of us have the natural skill that it takes to be a mistake-proofing expert to one degree or another. All that is required is a little training. The training is not expensive and does not require greatly specialized skills to conduct. In fact, the training is more awareness oriented than anything else. Pick someone in the organization with a great deal of common sense and send him or her off to a seminar to become a trainer on the subject. Or kick start the initiative by bringing in an experienced trainer to train 20 people or so in a day or two. You may even choose to do both, or you may hire an experienced trainer and then select an in-house trainer from the first group of 20 employees you train. Again, pick someone with good common sense who wants the job and is well respected by others in the facility. When the training method has been selected and the trainer is in place, train everyone. The more employees looking for ways to permanently eliminate errors, the quicker the organization will arrive at an error free environment, or at least close to an error free environment.

The training should be formal in that it is scheduled and mandatory, yet it should be kept informal in that everyone should be encouraged to participate in the training activity. Pure and simple, make this a condition of employment. New employees should be scheduled to take the course as part of their orientation. If new employees are hired infrequently, the new employee training can be postponed until enough students are available. However, don't put off training the new employees too long. If new employee contributions are to be maximized, train them early; a fresh set of eyes can see opportunities that have been missed by your current employees. "The longer you are in the presence of a problem, the less likely you are to solve it." – Maurice Nicol.

Examples of Mistake Proofing

As part of the course, each student will be called upon to draw on his or her own every day life experiences. As mentioned in an earlier chapter, everyone has had many encounters with examples of mistake proofing; some more examples are listed as follows:

- The second drain hole on a bathroom sink that prevents water overflow
- Child proof locks in the home and car
- Circuit breakers
- Automatic seat belts
- Automatic lights
- Electric eyes on elevator doors
- Grocery store scanners
- Self-cleaning ovens that lock when cleaning
- The camera that will not allow a picture to be taken if lens cover is not removed

In addition to mistake proofing encountered every day, many examples can be found in the workplace. Some examples are listed below:

- Double switches on machinery that require both hands be occupied, so that a hand cannot be placed in harm's way when the machine is operating.
- Bar code scanners that eliminate keying errors all too common in keyboard entry.

- Relationship database – these databases compare an actual set of data to a stored predetermined set of desired data that should be achieved under the given circumstances.
- Photo sensors that detect anything foreign in a path and send a warning or prevent an action.
- Automatic "on—off" timers.
- Notched parts that can only fit one way.
- Shaped parts that match the same shape receptacle, allowing only one orientation on contact.
- Test equipment that senses DIP switch settings and will not allow the process to continue until the desired settings are present.
- Circuit board in-circuit testers that exercise the circuit and can check for shorts (opens), component orientation, component presence and component values.
- Templates that prevent picking the wrong parts for a specific product build – the template covers the bins of parts not needed on the current build and only allows access to the components required.
- Tools and fixtures that seat themselves on set up.
- Scales that check counts.
- Interlocked doors that cannot be opened when another door is open, i.e., in a darkroom where double doors are used to keep out light; when one door is opened, the other door is automatically locked.
- Serial number comparative database that will not allow duplicates, similar to a relationship database: if the number has been used before, it has been stored in the database and cannot be used again.

Levels of Mistake Proofing

There are two levels of mistake proofing. The first level (the lower level) makes it easier to recognize when an error is about to occur or an error has just occurred. An example of mistake proofing that makes it easier to recognize when an error is about to occur is the warning buzzer that warns you your keys are about to be left in your car's ignition. These are based primarily on warning alert signals. An example of mistake proofing that makes it easier to recognize that an error has occurred is the tray that contains a cotter pin, which was supposed to go into the subassembly that was just passed on to the next manufacturing stage. The container would be empty when the next set up was prepped, if the cotter pin had been used on the previous assembly. In this case the operator places in the container just the parts required to build one subassembly, prior to starting the assembly process. If any parts remain in the bins after the previous subassembly is completed, they will be detected at this, the set up point. It is at this point that it becomes obvious that a part has been left out of the previous assembly. These are the least desirable mistake proofing methods, in that an error can still occur. The next level is the most desirable.

The second level (the higher level) of mistake proofing, the most desirable, is prevention of an error from occurring. With these methods the process is designed not to allow an error to occur. The process may shut down if an error is about to occur, or the design of the mistake proofing will simply not permit an error to occur. As one progresses from the lower levels to the higher levels of mistake proofing, the manufacturing process is progressively less dependent on the Operator for error free performance. An example of these mistake proofing methods is the final test equipment that will not allow the final test to be completed unless the DIP switches are set exactly as the software just downloaded into the final assembly being tested dictates. Another is the notched component that simply will only fit one way in the assembly, or the component that will work no matter which way it is inserted in the assembly. These types of mistake proofing solutions permanently resolve your mistake causing issues by not allowing mistakes to occur.

Often when a higher level solution is not immediately evident, it makes sense to implement a lower level solution first that provides a warning that a mistake is about to occur or has occurred, to be followed at a later date by a better solution on the next, higher level, that will not allow a mistake to occur. An excellent example of this is the Test equipment above that will not allow the test to be completed unless the DIP switches are set correctly. The first real life iteration of this mistake proofing process just presented a picture on the display of how the DIP switches would look if they were set correctly, alongside another picture of the way the DIP switches were actually currently set. The theory was, the Test Operator, seeing how the switches were supposed to be set next to an image of how they were actually set, would fix the problem. In fact, it cured 98 percent of the problems, but we were after a 100 percent fix. The next higher level of mistake proofing, preventing the test from being completed, came later and was the 100 percent fix we were looking for. The important thing to remember is, when you find a lower level solution, keep looking for that solution that completely eliminates errors by preventing them altogether.

Tools and Methods of Mistake Proofing

The tools and methods of mistake proofing are many and varied. The only limits are the extent of the creative abilities and imaginations of the individuals doing the mistake proofing. Cost can also be a limiting factor. However, if one method is too costly, find another, less costly method that gets you close to a 100 percent solution. Sometimes the method that is chosen may not be the most desirable, yet may be the only one affordable. Some of

Quality and Mistake Proofing (Poka-yoke)

the various tools and methods are listed here; this list is by no means intended to be a complete list:

- Motion detectors – checking for movement or presence
- Contact devices – checking for presence, position or orientation
- Trip lights – checking for position
- Fit for function – notching or shaping for orientation
- Comparative databases – checking for the equivalent or the nonequivalent
- Scales – checking for presence, volume or size
- Using components as conductors that power equipment
- Counters – checking quantity for presence
- Pass through holes – checking for size
- Photo cells – checking for presence, size or quantity, or quality
- Colors – simple form identification
- Control Charts – allow for control of the process
- Templates – ensure access to correct items

The Fun Factor

One of the nicest parts of mistake proofing is that it is fun work. No engineering degree is required, only common sense. Everyone can get into the act. The next blockbuster idea can come from anyone. Employees from all levels of the organization and all walks of life get to work together resolving problems. This will lower costs and improve quality; what a great way to apply an employee's talents and energy!

Summary

The purpose of mistake proofing is to minimize the possibility of a workmanship error through the use of warnings, or to completely eliminate workmanship errors through the "fool proofing" (Poka-yoke) of processes, making work virtually error free. Mistake proofing is based on simple technology that can be easily grasped with a little training. By applying common sense solutions that seek to permanently fix everyday problems which arise in the workplace, processes become free of errors, making expensive inspections unnecessary and eliminating costly scrap and rework. No engineering degree is required, only common sense. Employees from all levels of the organization and all walks of life get to work together resolving problems with solutions that will lower costs and improve quality.

CHAPTER 20

Quality and Out-of-Box Failure Elimination

Out-of-Box Failures are evil. The worst way to present your product to your Customers is through an Out-of-Box Failure. Always assume you have only one chance to prove your product to its buyers. Imagine you are the Customer and you buy one item from a supplier. You open the box, take the product out, plug it in, turn it on, and it doesn't work. Having purchased only one item from the supplier, as far as you are concerned from your experience, everything the supplier makes is a defect. You may or may not give the supplier another chance. If a second chance is denied, the Customer/Supplier relationship is terminated, maybe forever. You will not keep your Customers very long, if you ship them Out-of-Box Failures (OBFs).

Your goal should be to eliminate Out-of-Box Failures forever from your business. Form a Team and include members from the highest levels of your business to deal with this issue. The Team members should be cross functional. Draw them from areas like Engineering, Manufacturing, Manufacturing Engineering, Quality Assurance/Regulatory Affairs, and Sourcing. Preferably the heads of these groups will make up the Team members. It is necessary that the representatives from these key areas have the clout necessary to devote whatever resources are needed to address and fix problems as they arise. Meet at regularly scheduled times and demand that anyone not able to be present send an alternate with the authority to make commitments. Review each and every Out-of-Box Failure. If technical expertise is required, a technician should review each failure prior to the meeting. The technician can either submit a written report summarizing his or her findings to the Team members, or he or she can be present at the meeting. Keep accurate records of all products reviewed, spelling out corrective actions and follow-up on any corrective actions that arose out of previous meetings, until all actions are complete.

Break the failures down into four categories. The first category and the most difficult to fix is the "no problem found" category. When this occurs, your Customer perceives that there is a problem and you cannot identify the problem. Second, and the next most difficult to fix, is the "random component failure" category. This is the totally random failure of a purchased component such as a capacitor or resistor. Third, and an easier problem to fix than the previous two, is the "Engineering failure" category. These failures arise either because of a flaw in the design or a failure mode that could have been prevented with a better design. Fourth, and the easiest failures to fix, are those caused by "poor workmanship." These are the easiest to fix because you have complete control. You can revise procedures, retrain employees, implement "mistake proofing" solutions, etc., eliminating the possibility of errors from future shipments. These four failure modes are where you should focus your efforts on eliminating all Out-of-Box Failures from your business.

"No problem found," as I said previously, is the most difficult type of problem to solve. The Customer involved believes he or she has a defective product and returns the product as an Out-of-Box Failure. You can't find anything wrong with the product. If the problem is intermittent, persistence may duplicate the condition causing the failure, which can in turn lead to a permanent resolution of the problem. However, a "no problem found" Out-of-Box Failure can be caused by situations beyond your immediate control. There could be a problem with the "users training" your Customer received. Improper installation by the Customer can cause the failures. The product can be misused or used for a purpose for which the product was not intended. Other Customer-owned equipment that works with your equipment might be the cause of the problem. In one actual scenario, my equipment continually failed in one particular large and prestigious hospital. After quite a lengthy investigation, our service folks were able to determine that the voltage being supplied to the equipment from the hospital's own power supply was the cause of the problem. Installing some simple controlling devices fixed the problem. When complaints are limited to one area or one Customer or even one group of Customers, this is a signal to look for a problem that is peculiar to that situation, such as the one cited here.

"Random component failures" are usually caused by a purchased component. The cause may not necessarily be the vendor's fault. Your product may be pushing the component to its limit. Although the component will work well in your equipment under most circumstances, the component may fail under certain unusual or infrequent conditions. The fix is usually to replace the component with a more robust component with higher or wider tolerances. If the failure is caused by a defect supplied by your vendor, the Out-of-Box Failure Team should request a corrective action plan from the vendor and follow up on the corrective action request until the request is satisfied. Other alternatives are to replace the vendor, or in the case of a commercially available component, replace the component with another manufacturer's product. Also, a redesign may be required to eliminate, replace or add another component, such as a resistor, to cure the failure mode. Because you usually lack direct control over your vendors' manufacturing processes, this failure mode is more difficult to deal with than the next two.

Engineering failures are failures that should have or could have been prevented by a change in design. Also lumped into this category will be failures which fall under any of the other three categories that can be eliminated through an Engineering action. Remember, to make great progress in this area, the players must not be defensive. There is no room for thin-skinned Team members trying to defend their turf. There can be no finger pointing and no witch-hunts, trying to assign blame. The Team must focus on only one lofty goal, the complete elimination of Out-of-Box Failures. Design flaws don't always show up early in a product's life cycle. The commercial component that delivered good results for a short period of time could have morphed into a non-functioning component because of a change in the manufacturer's process. This is not an uncommon occurrence with commercial electronics, especially commercially available printed circuit boards and computer accessories. These issues should be caught before arriving at the Customer site for installation; however, the testing currently being done on your end items is based on known parameters. When those parameters suddenly change, they are easy to miss in your product's final testing. This is one reason an aggressive Out-of-Box Failure program is so important. It will permit you to redefine your final testing to catch these types of problems that sometimes seem to come out of nowhere.

"Workmanship failures" are the easiest to fix, and because of this fact, these are the best problems to have. If you have to have any problems, vote for problems in this category. These are the easiest failures to identify and you have the most control over preventing this type of failure. Most frequently the problems can be fixed with a little training. Then there is always the opportunity to mistake proof the process (find a Poka-yoke solution). See the Chapter on mistake proofing. A full-time trainer can ensure that the employees maintain a high level of manufacturing skill. The trainer will be tied into the Out-of-Box Failure process, primarily looking for candidates that can use further training. Again, be careful: no witch hunting, the goal is to surface, define and fix the problems, not to cast blame. You will lose the cooperation of your workforce, if the Out-of-Box Failure workmanship retraining is not handled professionally.

Insist on the return of all Out-of-Box Failures to the location that manufactured the product. A proper analysis of all Out-of-Box Failures is a must to any successful Out-of-Box Failure Elimination program. Accept no excuses here in getting the product back. There are really only two choices here: either bring the product back to the factory or fly the entire OBF Team to the Customer's site. DO NOT let your Field Service personnel repair the equipment and report the problem back to the factory. Allowing the Field Service folks to repair an Out-of-Box Failure introduces another variable; this may postpone indefinitely the finding of a permanent solution to correct the failure mode and prevent future unhappy Customers. Also, Field Service personnel, when installing products, may even cause failures. If they are allowed to repair the item they installed, this failure mode will go undetected and untreated. There is no substitute for a dissection of the failure back home in the factory by the people who are responsible for designing and building the product. This may mean that the Customer has to be provided with another piece of equipment while theirs is under repair. Depending on the type of product being sold, the returned product after adjustment or repair may be able to be resold as new. By definition an Out-of-Box Failure was never used — it failed before use and was returned, so by definition it is not a used product. Also, many businesses have Customer requirements for used equipment; this may be an opportunity to make a Customer happy with a "new-used" piece of equipment at a nice discount.

Winning in a Highly Competitive Manufacturing Environment

When evaluating a returned product, it may be very advantageous to talk directly to the Customer who experienced the failure. Many Sales or Distribution folks object to factory personnel talking directly to their Customer. Allow the Sales person to be on the call, if you feel this is appropriate, but make the call under any circumstances — its vital to the future of the business. The Customer can be essential to finding the problem and the solution, especially when there is a "no problem found" issue involved. Any direct contact with the Customer can be turned into a good relations building opportunity. Many Customer relationships are strengthened because of a failure problem with a product. The Customer will not be as put off by an Out-of-Box Failure, if the Customer receives the right attention immediately. Make sure that the factory folks dealing directly with the Customers understand these basic principals.

When necessary, the Team as a group should personally dissect the "no problem found" and any other persistent problem units with or without a Technician. There is one situation that comes to mind here. This took place when one of my companies found itself dealing with a rash of "no problem found" Out-of-Box Failures. The entire Team – Director of Engineering, Quality Assurance Manager, Regulatory Affairs Manager, Manufacturing Manager, Sourcing Manager, Manufacturing Engineering Manager and Vice President of Operations – poured over every "no problem found" Out-of-Box Failure. By doing a "deep dive" on each unit, the Team resolved an issue that turned many "no problem found" units into identified failures. The elusive problem was found when the Director of Engineering asked to see the piece of equipment that the failed unit had been configured with. All seemed to be in order: the equipment sported a brand new Calibration sticker showing that the equipment had recently been calibrated and the Operator was using the equipment correctly. Next the Team followed the Director of Engineering to the Calibration Lab, where he asked to be shown the calibration procedure. Bingo! The wrong procedure was being used. Problem identified and fixed early before any more units were shipped to our Customers. This kind of devotion to problem solving, leading to Out-of-Box Failure elimination by the Management Team, sets the right example for the entire organization. The message is that the elimination of Out-of-Box Failures is a number one priority, essential to the business's success.

One type of Out-of-Box Failure which should never occur deserves mention here. That is the "short shipment." Perhaps this is the most sinful failure because it is so easily prevented. As far as your Customer is concerned, if he does not receive everything he needs to operate the item he purchased, the product is defective. To eliminate this failure mode, simply never ship a partial shipment to a Customer unless the Customer has agreed to accept an incomplete shipment. Stand fast to this rule even at the end-of-the month, end-of-the quarter and end-of-the year. Your Customers will be grateful and your business will be stronger for not using this crutch.

Finally, where Out-of-Box Failures are concerned, all reporting should be formal. In addition to complying with any legal requirements your business may have, a method of tracking the types of failures and the Customers involved will allow for tracking of developing trends. Spotting a developing trend can help identify failure modes that would not be easily spotted without the trend tracking. Also keep formal records for each corrective action issued internally to Manufacturing or Engineering and externally to a Supplier. Review the records and go after any past due requested corrective actions, either from your own folks or your vendors. Publish summary reports and post them in locations where everyone who touches the product will see them. And lastly, don't forget to celebrate the successes.

Summary

The worst way to present your product to your Customers is through an Out-of-Box Failure. Always assume you have only one chance to prove your product to its buyers. Imagine you are the Customer and you buy only one item from a Supplier. You open the box, take the product out, plug it in, turn it on and it doesn't work. Your goal should be to eliminate Out-of-Box Failures forever from your business. Out-of-Box Failures fall into four categories: First, "no problem found" – your Customer perceives that there is a problem and you cannot identify the problem. Second, "random component failures" – these are the totally random failures of a purchased component such as a capacitor or resistor. Third, "Engineering failures" – these failures arise either because of a flaw in the design or a failure mode that could have been prevented with a better design. Fourth, "poor workmanship" – these failures are caused by human error. Form a Cross-Functional Team and include members from the highest levels of your business to deal with this issue, using the process improvement tools previously discussed in this book.

PART 4
TEAMS

CHAPTER 21

Cross-Functional Self-Directed Teams

So, how do we get all the things we have talked about in the previous chapters accomplished in a short amount of time without hiring tons of additional personnel to manage the initiatives? Simple, we can use the talent we already have in place to accomplish our goals by using "Cross-Functional Self-Directed" work Teams to execute many of our new initiatives. By making the Teams Cross-Functional, we draw on the various talents across the organization. These talents should be germane to the initiative to be addressed by the Team. For instance, if we are forming a Team that will address inventory reduction, someone from Sourcing should be on the Team and someone from Logistics, along with the Master Scheduler. It is usually wise to draw from the bargaining unit, if a Union is in place in the facility. Having a Team that crosses functional lines is expedient in that it will make available the diversity of talent that is usually required to address the initiatives, which touch more than one area of the business. Another benefit derived from forming a Cross-Functional Team is its ability to eliminate resistance and break down barriers at the grassroots level. By including as Team members, individuals who are respected by their peers, the Team's ideas will be more readily accepted – the Team sells their ideas to their fellow employees whom they interface with routinely. It may even be a good idea to include an individual on the Team who is believed to be resistant to the type of change being promoted. Eliminating resistance through Team membership is an excellent way to create a convert, and converts will become the project zealots. Another good reason for forming a Cross-Functional Team is that it makes it easy to draw on the resources from an area of the business when one of the Team members is working in that area. Information Technology assistance is easier to secure, if the person asking for the assistance is an employee from the Information Technology end of the business.

In addition to being "Cross-Functional," the Team is "Self-Directed." Self-Directed means just that: Self-Directed. Most of us cannot rely on only ourselves to accomplish major initiatives. It is usually necessary to draw on the talents of the people who surround us. The Team concept is far more effective without a dominating personality being present. Optimum Team performance is fostered when all Team members participate equally in the Team process, and when all Team members feel that their opinions are important, they will give them freely. The senior member of Management forming the Team should pick the Team Leader and Team Facilitator and then, together with these individuals, pick a few candidates for Team membership. At the first Team meeting after the Team has been formed, the Senior Manager forming the Team will address the Team to deliver the challenge. After the Team challenge has been delivered, this individual leaves the Team meeting, not to return unless invited by the Team. Great care must be used by Management not to interfere with the Self-Directed Team's work. This may even mean biting one's tongue and accepting what you believe to be mistakes, in the interest of non-interference. Once an outsider with the power to interfere and usurp the Team's authority does so, you no longer have a Self-Directed Team. If things are so bad that interference is absolutely necessary, request an invitation to address the Team and lay out your concerns. Make the Team understand that they are the decision makers. Your guest appearance is just to make suggestions that the Team may elect to ignore. If your guest appearance fails to gain the desired results and greater interference is warranted, disband the Team and start over. At this point, using your influence will neuter the Team anyway, so just start over with a fresh Team. Remember, responsibility, accountability and authority go together; you can't have one without the other two. A policy of non-interference will make your Self-Directed Teams a powerful force in your business.

One of my actual experiences with a "Cross-Functional Self-Directed Team" that didn't take my advice led me to allow the Team to spend a few thousand dollars more than they had to. OK, I'll say it – waste a few thousand dollars. (Oh, that still hurts.) The "Automated Data Collection Team," when in the process of setting up the circuit board manufacturing area for a new data collection system, insisted on installing too many bar code readers and printers. The Team wanted to place a reader and printer at the birthing station. This is the station that adds the bar code to the raw board, giving it identity, and starts the clock ticking for the cycle time measurements for most products. The Team also wanted readers at the DIP inserter, axial inserter, random component locators, wave solder machine and aqueous cleaner. I requested and was granted an audience with the Team. I expressed my concern, telling the Team that when this area was converted to a flow manufacturing cell, which was another Team effort taking place at the same time, there would be no need for so many readers because the circuit boards would not be in the area long enough. The Team was playing the game under the current rules where circuit boards remained in the area for weeks, not days or hours. I was drawing on my previous experiences, which told me that soon the crippling shortage situation would be cured and boards would no longer take weeks to move through this area; it would take less than two days from the birthing station to the end of the board line. I was eventually proven correct, but not before the Team purchased and installed every reader and printer they originally wanted installed. Obviously the Team was unmoved by my argument that the circuit boards would be moving so quickly through the area that the extra equipment would not be needed. They had lived for so many years with the shortage problems that they could not comprehend what life would be like without the shortages: their past experience dictated their actions.

I believe two things were going on in the above situation. First, the Team did believe that the equipment was needed. Second, the Team was testing to see if Management really meant what it said about the Teams being Self-Directed. Four different "Cross-Functional Self-Directed" Teams had been simultaneously kicked off and this was the first test. If I had, at this early stage of Team empowerment, over- ruled the Team on its decision to purchase the equipment, the success of all the Teams would have been jeopardized. It was far better to spend a few extra thousand dollars making an investment in the Team process than to undermine the Team's authority. Management gave the Teams the responsibility; Management intended to hold the Teams accountable. It was necessary for Management to reaffirm the Team's authority. All four Teams went on to be very successful, saving this company millions of dollars. The extra equipment was a good investment.

Influencing the Team

There are several ways for the Team's creator to influence the Team's performance. The first will be through the Team Leader and the Team Facilitator, both of whom the Team's creator appointed when the Team was formed. The Team will generate minutes of each meeting. The minutes will be distributed not only to the Team members, but also the Team's creator. In this

Cross-Functional Self-Directed Teams

way the Team creator will know what direction the Team is heading in. It is acceptable for the Team creator to attempt to influence both the Team Leader and the Team Facilitator. The Facilitator should be skilled in dealing with conflict and have the ability to deal with any conflicts that may arise in a professional manner. The Team creator, knowing that conflicts may arise between what the Team perceives is in the best interests of the organization and what Management perceives is in the best interests of the organization, should pick the Facilitator carefully.

Another way for Management to influence the Team is to set a date and call for a Team presentation. A very important element contributing to the success of the "Cross-Functional Self-Directed" Team concept is the Team presentation. The Team should be required to give periodic presentations to a member of the senior Management Team on a regular basis. The stated purpose of the presentation will be to update Management on the Team's progress. The unstated purpose is to keep pressure on the Team to continue to make progress toward meeting the Team challenge. No one wants to get up in front of his or her Management during the presentation and confess that the Team has not made any progress. There is a great deal of pressure from the Teammates themselves to "get stuff done" before the presentation date so that the Team can look good to Management.

If the previous Team influencing methods are unsuccessful at moving the Team in the desired direction, the Team creator can request an invitation to attend a regular Team meeting or even call a special Team meeting. These should be very rare occasions. Too many of these requested audiences and you no longer have a Self-Directed Team. Present your best case to the Team, making them understand that you are not dictating to them, but also making it clear that you are trying to influence their decision, then leave the meeting while the Team considers your suggestions.

In addition to the above, you can always count on human nature. There is usually an inclination for the Team to want to please the Team creator. So make your positions known. Keep the lines of communications between senior Management and the Team open, upfront and honest. The Team will appreciate Management giving them free rein in meeting the challenge. They will be inclined to please.

Team Training

Soon after forming each new Team, provide the entire Team with formal Team training. Many human resource leaders have had experience with Team training. If you have no one who can provide Team training inside your organization, this type of training is readily available through various human resource organizations.

The training should cover the various stages of Team development that most Teams go through, from the kickoff stage through the productive stage. This will help the members understand what to expect in their interactions with their fellow Teammates. Other topics should include:

- Why governance is important.
- An understanding of what is expected of the Team Leader, the Team Facilitators and the Team members.
- An explanation of how the Team Leader's role changes as the Team matures. (The Team Leader assumes more of a Team Member's role as the Team matures and leadership is not as necessary as it was when the Team was first formed.)

No role is more important here than the Team Facilitator's role. Unless the Team Facilitator already has had experience and training in this role, it would be wise to provide facilitator training to the individuals serving in this role. Although a full member of the Team, the role of facilitator is unique in that his or her first responsibility is to the Team process itself. I usually try to get the Team facilitators from the Human Resource group. These folks make good facilitators because they are far enough removed from the routine day-to-day plant activities. A good Team facilitator recognizes that their first responsibility is to monitor the Team process. The closer an individual is to the problem at hand, the more difficult it becomes to monitor the Team process. A trained facilitator should promote and encourage participation by all Team members, run interference with upper Management, maintain fairness, help create a sense of harmony, keep the Team spirit alive, help settle internal disputes, recommend new Team members, and encourage the celebration of successes.

The Team Challenge

The Team challenge should be easy to understand, measurable, have a time limit and be relevant to the business's success. It should be a stretch to achieve, yet achievable. Some actual examples of Team challenges follow:

- *Reduce inventory by $10,000,000 by the end of the year. This was the goal of an Inventory Reduction Team. The Team was very successful. They started with $24,000,000 in inventory and successfully reduced that inventory to $14,000,000. In actuality there were three distinct inventory Teams in this same company, serving in succession. The three Teams eventually drove inventory down to $7,000,000, while at the same time top line revenue doubled, making the inventory investment work more than six times harder than it had prior to the Teams' work.*

The second inventory reduction Team was formed after the first Team was disbanded, and the third Team was formed after the second Team was disbanded. A "Cross-Functional Self-Directed" Team should be disbanded with celebration when it has met its challenge. If this were not the case, the Teams would go on forever, tying up valuable resources that should be focused elsewhere. Three different Teams were required because, although the goal of reducing inventory was common to all three Teams, the methods they had to use to achieve their goals were quite different. Hence, three different Teams were composed of people with different talents, able to deal with the different issues facing each of the three Teams. For instance, the first inventory Team focused on issues like selling used inventory equipment, reworking unusable inventory into usable inventory, then selling it, and returning unneeded material to the vendors who supplied it or pushing off material deliveries by rescheduling Purchase Orders. There were Team members from Sales and Marketing to help move the inventory, as well as members from Manufacturing and Manufacturing Engineering to help figure out how to repair and rework unusable inventory into usable inventory. By the time the last of the three inventory Teams started their work, they were focusing on things like reducing the size of the material Kanbans and integrating assemblies into production cells. The makeup of the final Team didn't include any members from Sales or Marketing; its membership centered on the supply chain.

- *Improve on-time delivery hit rate to the 99% + level over the next year. This Team was coming from so far back that it actually took almost a year and a half to satisfy the challenge. On-time delivery was at 53% when the Team challenge was delivered. Also, some of the late orders were weeks late, not just a few days. The Company was shipping more than 10,000 line items a month to virtually every hospital in the United States and many outside the USA. An order was considered on time if it was shipped prior to the promised ship date. No tolerance window was allowed. If the order was one minute late, it was counted as late. Prior to the Team measuring the on-time delivery for the first time, this Company didn't even know how bad its delivery rate was.*

Cross-Functional Self-Directed Teams

The Team's members came from the various areas of the Company that had the most influence over on-time delivery, including: Order Entry, Customer Service, Sales, Shipping/Logistics, Sourcing, and Manufacturing, and the Facilitator was the Human Resources Manager. These Team members addressed and improved a variety of issues that were causing late deliveries, such as: unrealistic promises to Customers, late vendor deliveries causing late builds, priority setting, freight carrier selection, short shipments, order entry errors and Customer ordering errors.

When the Team was disbanded, they left behind a strong infrastructure that would build on their successes for years to come. Eventually, on-time delivery was defined as the date the Customer requested the delivery at the Customer's site. This is a much tougher method of measuring on-time delivery, basing your performance on the date the Customer wants the delivery, rather than on the date you promised the delivery. When you know you are being measured, you tend to pad the delivery promise. With the new tougher measure the Customer can be unreasonable and the measurement stands – meet the request and you are on time, miss the request and you are late. Also, early shipments were not allowed and partial shipments were not allowed.

- *Eliminate the use of Shop Floor Work Orders by December. This Team was really the Flow Manufacturing Team. It was not called the Flow Manufacturing Team or the Just-in-Time Team because a few years before, this same Company had a failed attempt at implementing Just-in-Time. The memories of that failed event were so negative that often during group discussions with the employees they would point out the failure, always saying that they hoped the Company would never make that mistake again. Hence, The "Work Order Elimination" Team. A few weeks after the Team was formed, the Team Leader came to see me. He said the Team had been doing quite a bit of thinking about the Team* challenge, and that they had decided the only real way to eliminate Work Orders completely was through Just-in-Time flow manufacturing. By that time, the Team was so far into the problem that they were accepting of their fate. They still kept the old name of "The Work Order Elimination Team." In 10 months the Team had completely eliminated Work Orders from the Shop Floor. They had started with over 1,100 work orders.

The Team members were drawn from: Manufacturing, Materials Planning, Sourcing, Manufacturing Engineering, Logistics and Accounting. The Facilitator was a representative from Human Resources. On this Team the representative from Accounting was key to the success of the program. It was the Accounting Team member's responsibility to sell the idea to the Finance folks and work out the new methods to collect and account for material and labor costs. It was on this Team's successes that this company built its entire flow manufacturing system.

- *Automate the data collection system on the manufacturing floor – have the new system up and running by January 1. This Team suffered through three different leaders. The first died, the second quit and the third remained until the Team was disbanded. This Team effort not only suffered through three different Team Leaders, it was a victim of project creep. No sooner was the Team about to wrap-up the original project and declare the challenge met, than the parent Company decided to implement a new global system. Of course, this meant that much of the original interface work with the current system had to be done over. It was felt that the Team in place was the closest to the issues and would have the best chance at succeeding with the interface to the new ERP system. Many new requirements were added to the specification to take advantage of the new system's capabilities. The software that the Team had originally selected did not play well with the new system, leading to several ugly work around solutions. None of these difficulties were the fault of the Team; however, their spirits

Cross-Functional Self-Directed Teams

were dampened and the work dragged on with little to celebrate. Eventually the Team delivered on most of the requirements, but it took years – far too long for a "Self-Directed" Team. In retrospect, it would have been far better to sacrifice any benefit derived from the Team's experience with the first iteration of the automated data collection system and start a new Team with the introduction of the global ERP system. A valuable lesson for all involved to remember.

Team membership included representation from Manufacturing, Quality Assurance/Regulatory Affairs, Manufacturing Engineering, Materials, Engineering, Accounting, Sourcing, Shipping/Logistics, and again the Facilitator was selected from Human Resources. This Team had a very large membership of a dozen members. The specialized knowledge each Team Member had in their respective areas dictated the need for a large Team. Also, as this system's effect was far reaching in the organization, the Team's membership was drawn from those many areas most affected, in an effort to assure buy in.

One more thought on this Team: the presentations the Team delivered to top Management were superb. Initially the Team had an unbelievable amount of spirit. During one of the presentations delivered to the President of the Company and members of his Staff, the Team did a skit involving every member of the Team. The theme centered on the tons of paper that the Team would be eliminating from the Shop Floor. They collected one month's worth of paper and filled several carts. Wheeling the carts into the Conference Room drove home the importance of the Team's work. It was a very effective presentation.

- *Reduce burn-in time by 90,000 hours over the next year. This was the challenge of the Burn-in Reduction Team – another very successful Team. Most of the equipment built in this facility containing electronics was required to go through a burn-in process where the equipment was left running on a simulator, simulating operational conditions for three days at an elevated temperature. The theory was that stressing the equipment under these conditions would weed out the early failures. There are alternatives to this process. For instance, if you replace certain components that exhibit early failures with more robust components that do not exhibit early failures, you can eliminate the burn-in. In some cases, history can be used to prove that the burn-in period is no longer effective because there have been no failures for a sufficient length of time, say a year. The data may justify cutting back on the burn time, if not eliminating it altogether. Again, the product was medical equipment. Whenever the product being manufactured is a regulated product, great care must be taken to justify, validate and document the reasons for discontinuing any form of testing previously committed to, such as burn-in.*

The Team was made up mostly of Manufacturing Engineers, Quality Engineers and Test Engineers. In this case it was necessary to send a couple of Manufacturing Engineers to a Midwestern University to acquire the skills needed to implement, validate and document the burn-in reduction. The Team met its goal and was disbanded. This saved the Company hundreds of thousand of dollars in inventory that was tied up for days while being burned-in. The infrastructure the Team left behind continued to pay off for several years after the initial Team effort. As more products were moved to this factory from other factories by the parent company, they too went through the burn-in reduction process using the infrastructure the Burn-in Reduction Team left behind.

- *Reduce disposable manufacturing's work in process inventories by 50 percent and manufacturing floor space by 30 percent within the next year. This Team called itself the DOIT Team, which was an acronym for the Disposables Operations Improvement Team. This company had an extensive disposables manufacturing business. Many of the products manufactured here were sterilized using ethylene oxide. The working environment included a Clean Room as well as several other controlled environments. The Team delivered on the Team challenge in less than six months. The end result of the Team's efforts was a 50 percent reduction in work in process inventory, a 30 percent reduction in floor space, and a direct labor reduction of 1,500 hours a month which represented more than 25 percent of the total available monthly hours.*

This Team was made up mostly of employees who had been working in the Disposables manufacturing area for years and a few Manufacturing Engineers, as well as manufacturing Management. It was very important that we absorb the 1,500 hours a month that represented the labor saving efforts of the Team. Essentially, these Team members were eliminating their own jobs. Why would they do such a thing? The answer is simple: these cross-trained employees trusted that Management would use their skills elsewhere in the business. The Company was able to honor this unspoken commitment to these folks because of the overtime philosophy employed in running the operations end of the business. A lot of overtime had been worked in this area as well as other manufacturing areas of this factory. As these employees were cross-trained to perform several functions in other areas of the business, they were used to reduce the need for overtime in those areas. As a result, the 1,500 hours were absorbed. Working a fair amount of overtime in your facility gives you the flexibility to absorb the excess labor that results from this kind of innovation. All you have to do is replace some of the overtime with the excess labor created, provided, of course, that you have a well cross-trained workforce. Over a period of several years, after the introduction of flow manufacturing in this company, the company was occasionally faced with an excess labor problem. This was usually resolved through attrition and other techniques, such as encouraging employees to use their vacation during slow periods. Every effort should be made to keep your well-trained employees working during slow periods before resorting to a reduction in workforce, especially in circumstances such as those described above.

- *Eliminate all obsolete part numbers in the system within the next six months. This was the challenge of the "Part Number Elimination Team." This Team's job was to clean up the part number system that had been in effect for several decades by eliminating part numbers that were no longer needed because they were obsolete or in some cases duplicates. One characteristic that stood out with this Team was its ZEAL. The Team would routinely work through lunch performing the tedious tasks of investigating each part number that was a candidate for elimination. They would order pizzas and eat while they worked on their own time.*

Team Governance and Characteristics

I have listed below, with some elaboration, a few rules of governance and conduct that I have found successful in managing "Cross-Functional Self-Directed Teams" over the years.

- Team size should be more than 5 and less than 12. With less than five people you sacrifice the benefits of having a Cross-Functional or Self-Directed Team. Remember, one of the most powerful reasons for having such a Team is to gain acceptance in the affected areas. Use too few people and you give up something here. More than 12 Team members and the Team is too unwieldy. There are too many group dynamics going on. It just gets hard to keep anybody happy.

- Each Team is composed of a Team Leader – appointed; a Facilitator – appointed; a Secretary to keep minutes – elected; and the Team members – Invited or drafted. This is pretty self-explanatory, based on the previous discussions above.

Cross-Functional Self-Directed Teams

- The Team should meet at least once a week. Making this a ground rule forces the Team to meet and keep things moving. If the Team is meeting less than once a week, one has to question whether there is really a project going on or not. The first sign of trouble here will show up in the Team minutes or lack thereof.
- When a Team accomplishes its goals and the challenge has been met, the Team will be disbanded. If you have a project that requires a Team remain and continue in place, use a steering committee, not a "Cross-Functional Self-Directed" Team. The "Cross-Functional Self-Directed" Teams should be used to define and execute major projects, using the unique talents of the Team members. The work is usually over and above the Team member's everyday assignments; however, the challenge should be connected to the everyday work the Team member is normally assigned to. In fact, it is best if the Team member will be a beneficiary of the successful Team outcome.
- The Team must create an infrastructure that will survive the Team effort, so that the accomplishments of the Team will continue to bear fruit long after the Team has been disbanded. In several of the Team examples above, it was cited how the infrastructure that the Team left in place served the company well for years after. In fact, in many cases the infrastructure outperformed the Teams that created them. See in particular the on-time delivery Team and the burn-in Team discussed above.
- The Team sets goals and assigns tasks to meet the challenge. The Team creator establishes and delivers the challenge at the first Team meeting. However, the Team sets the goals that will have to be met to satisfy the challenge. In the case of a Self-Directed Team it would be counter productive and presumptuous for the creator to set the Team's

goals. The nature of the ongoing dynamics involved in the Teamwork will dictate changing goals as the Team progresses in its work. It would not be practical to have a Self-Directed Team and have the Team creator set the goals. This would negate the self-direction aspect of the Team.

- Each Team is empowered to draw on the talents and expertise available elsewhere in the company. This includes the entire organization. The talent would most likely be required on a part-time basis. For example, if help is required from the Sourcing Group to get vendor quotes, a buyer will be assigned to the Team until the quoting is complete. In this case it would make no sense for the Buyer to become a full Team member for the duration of the Team's existence, so a temporary assignment will serve the Team well. One note here: When the time comes to hand out the rewards for the Team's successes, don't forget to include the part timers proportionally to their efforts.

- Team meeting attendance and showing up on time are both important and mandatory in order to maintain Team membership. The Team must establish these ground rules early on, in the first or second meeting. It is a must that all Team members understand the rules. The entire Team must agree to the boundaries. Consequences for noncompliance must be established and adhered to. So many Teams fail to address these difficult issues at the outset, then a member starts missing meetings or letting the Team down in some way and the Team has no recourse. The Team creator should place a strong emphasis on the ground rules – setting needs at the kickoff meeting when the challenge is delivered. The Facilitator, especially if he or she is a Human Resources professional, can help with this process.

Cross-Functional Self-Directed Teams

One Team's actual experience involving a Team member who continually let the Team down, drove the Team to fire the individual from the Team. The individual served on a total of two Teams and, unfortunately, eventually the process was repeated with the other Team as well. Not long after being dismissed from the second Team, the individual left the company. These Teams both went on to become very successful despite this episode. The separation from the Team was handled professionally, partly because the mechanism was in place, having been dealt with at the Team's inception. The ability of the Team to terminate a Team member from the Team can be a powerful motivator. Most people would prefer to be fired by their company than to be fired by their peers.

- Teams are expected to give progress reports in the form of a presentation to a senior member of Management, the more senior, the better. The presentation helps to keep the project on track. It is the ultimate in Team pressure. The peer pressure to be prepared to deliver a good presentation is awesome. Nobody wants to go before top Management unprepared or with little to show for the Team's effort. This is the Team's opportunity to show off their abilities. They have a captive audience, a chance to get top Management to listen. I have seen wondrous things happen during Team presentations. There is some real give and take that goes on in these meetings. A Team needing additional resources may ask for Management's commitment, after trying to convince Management that the Team is worthy of further investment. It is impressive to see the effort that most Teams put into their presentations. They usually surprise on the upside with their command of the issues surrounding their project. Some of the presentations are on the light side, as discussed above with the Data Collection Team bringing a month's supply of paper to the presentation, representing the waste they were about to eliminate from the Shop Floor.

- Other governance ground rules should be established at the outset, at the first or second meeting, by the Team. We have already talked quite a bit about the importance of this action. Issues addressed should include items like missing meetings without an excuse, regularly being late for meetings, consequences, majority rule, open vote versus closed vote, level of expected effort, procedure for adding members or removing members, frequency of meetings and any other issues the Team deems necessary to cover. The Team creator should reinforce the importance of establishing these ground rules early. He should explain that although it is hoped that the mutual respect the Team members have for each other will be enough to resolve any issues that come up, it is a good business practice to formalize the ground rules governing Team activities and behavior, if only to avoid any misunderstanding.

Team Celebrations and Awards

Celebrations are a great way to say thanks and encourage more of the same results that will bring more celebrations. Celebrate even the small successes. They can be a simple cake and coffee break or a pizza party. The acknowledgement for a job well done is the important thing. Just say thanks. Companies with more resources can do more – cash awards, gift certificates, etc.

In addition to the minor celebrations along the Team's path to meeting the challenge, one of my companies gave each Team member a $1,000 cash award and the Team leader received $1,500 for his or her efforts. This in no way was meant as compensation for the work they had done. In most cases it would not have amounted to 50 cents an hour in compensation for all the extra hours the Team members put in on the projects. The awards were a way to say thanks for their efforts. It was as much a bonus for their spouses, who sacrificed while their husbands or wives worked overtime. On one occasion several members from one Team in Connecticut were asked to spend Valentine's Day in Milwaukee, Wisconsin. The Team Leader had roses sent to the Team members' spouses back in Connecticut. What a hit that was! They talked about that gesture for months. Another Team had the Company cafeteria prepare dinners to be taken home for the spouses of the Team members who had to work late on a project. This only cost the Company a few dollars each and demonstrated to the Team members' families that the company recognized and was appreciative of the sacrifice the whole family was making. It made the employees look like heroes in their families' eyes.

Some Teams would give away leather binders with the Team name on the cover. Others would have ball caps or jackets. This was a way for the Team members to build Team spirit, identify and be identified with the Team. Evening mystery cruises, dinner theatre tickets, baseball tickets – you name it and these Teams did it. They worked hard and had fun doing it.

Benefits of "Cross-Functional Self-Directed" Teams

One of the nicest benefits of forming "Cross-Functional Self-Directed" Teams is their ability to break down traditional barriers between departments. Team members are placed in situations where they have to rely and depend on each other's talents and skills to succeed as a Team. There is nothing like these types of situations to harvest respect for fellow employees. Just becoming familiar with a co-worker's responsibilities and daily challenges brings an understanding between individuals and groups. Development of mutual respect is a natural byproduct of an entire Team drawn from different areas of the business, pulling in the same direction to achieve a common goal.

Improving communications is another Team benefit. Communications between individuals and organizations can't help but improve when fellow employees sit next to each other working on a common goal. Remember, the Team must meet at least once a week.

The "Cross-Functional Self-Directed" Teams will Foster camaraderie, and the goodwill created will far outlast the Teams or their efforts. After all, many have learned a new common lingo through their Teamwork. The friendships and relationships developed through the Teamwork will spill over into the other day-to-day activities in the rest of the business. Some of the relationships between employees even spill over into their personal lives. In some of my companies there were very strong personal relationships that continued for years after the Team effort was over. In one case, a Team member became a Godparent to a fellow Teammate's child. At another company a Team helped a single mother Teammate fix up and move into a new home. They joined professional organizations together and some went to school together nights.

Employees develop a sense of ownership when asked to resolve a major issue that deeply affects the company's success. The project becomes their baby. They want to see that nothing adverse happens that will negatively affect their baby. And, of course, when a Team member gets close to a project, they are getting closer to the entire company. The more they have invested in a company, the keener they are about the health of that company.

We end up with better, longer lasting improvements that are implemented much more quickly. With limited resources, where does a company get the talent they need to run the day-to-day business while at the same time making great improvements on a grand scale? The answer is the "Cross-Functional Self-Directed" Team.

No Work Happens Until the Tool Hits the Material

Use these Teams to get the work done. One thing I remember from my college physics classes – no work happens until the tool hits the material. You get up in the morning, shower, dress, eat breakfast and drive to your place of work. You may get a cup of coffee. Collect your tools or lay out the work you need to do in front of you. Up to this point, NO WORK HAS HAPPENED. Not until you pick up the tool – be it pencil, pen or screwdriver — and touch it to the material – be it paper or Phillips-head screw – has any work happened. Once the tool has touched the material, then you can claim that work has happened. Your "Cross-Functional Self-Directed" Teams are your tools. Your challenges are their work. Your job as creator is to bring them together.

Summary

The "Cross-Functional Self-Directed" Team is the vehicle we use to execute many of our new initiatives in a short amount of time without hiring tons of additional personnel. In this way we can use the talent we already have in place to accomplish our goals. By making the Teams Cross-Functional we draw on the various talents across the organization. Having a Team that crosses functional lines is expedient in that it will make available the diversity of talent that is usually required to address the initiatives which touch more than one area of the business, and at the same time eliminate resistance and break down barriers at the grassroots level. Self-Directed means just that: Self-Directed. Great care must be used by Management not to interfere with the Self-Directed Team's work. Once an outsider with the power to interfere and usurp the Team's authority does so, you no longer have a Self-Directed Team. Remember, responsibility, accountability and authority go together; you can't have one without the other two. A policy of non-interference will make your Self-Directed Teams a powerful force in your business.

Each Team is composed of a Team Leader – appointed; a Facilitator – appointed; a Secretary to keep minutes – elected; and the Team members – Invited or drafted. The Team challenge should be easy to understand, measurable, have a time limit and be relevant to the business's success. It should be a stretch to achieve, yet achievable.

There are several ways for the Team's creator to influence the Team's performance. The first will be through the Team Leader and the Team Facilitator, both of whom the Team's creator appointed when the Team was formed. The Team creator will be able to determine the direction the Team is heading in from the meeting minutes generated at each Team meeting. The Team creator, knowing that conflicts may arise between what the Team perceives is in the best interests of the organization and what Management perceives is in the best interests of the organization, should pick the Facilitator carefully. Another way for Management to influence the Team is the Team presentation to top Management. The stated purpose of the presentation will be to update Management on the Team's progress. The unstated purpose is to keep pressure on the Team to continue to make progress toward meeting the Team challenge. There is a great deal of pressure from the Teammates themselves to "get stuff done" before the presentation date so that the Team can look good to Management. If these Team-influencing methods are unsuccessful at moving the Team in the desired direction, the Team creator can request an invitation to attend a regular Team meeting or even call a special Team meeting in an attempt to directly influence the Team. Remember, the Team is Self-Directed and has the last word until it either meets the challenge or is disbanded.

Through the use of "Cross-Functional Self-Directed" Teams, we end up with better, longer lasting improvements that are implemented much more quickly. With limited resources, where does a company get the talent they need to run the day-to-day business, while at the same time making great improvements on a grand scale? The answer is the "Cross-Functional Self-Directed" Team. Your "Cross-Functional Self-Directed" Teams are your tools. Your challenges are their work. Your job as creator is to bring them together.

EPILOGUE: A FINAL WORD

We have covered a lot of ground in the 21 chapters of this undertaking. The intent was to walk the reader down a path that would lead to the creation of a new Millennium world class manufacturing company. The method used was simple language describing easy to understand ideas brought to life by relating real life examples that anyone in manufacturing could relate to. The best result that I can hope for is that I have sparked an interest in Lean-flow Manufacturing and continuous improvement techniques that will germinate into ideas leading to action. What has been written here is not just theory; it has been done over and over and it was great fun.

Remember: no work happens until the tool hits the material. Don't just put this book down and go back to doing business as usual. Take a look at your business; compare your own factory to the situations described in this book. Get your people involved through open, honest and up-front communication, as well as recognition and appreciation; this is an important key to gaining the trust that is required to carry out a Lean-flow Manufacturing continuous improvement program. Actions say more than words and your words must be backed by actions. I believe that your Company can achieve similar results or even greater results than those described in this book. Your employees can do it for you. Just ask them; they are ready to help.

Sources

Black, JT., *The Design of the Factory with a Future,* McGraw-Hill, Inc., New York, 1991.

Blanchard, Ken, Ph.D. Donald Carew, Ed.D., and Parisi-Carew, Eunice, Ed.D, *The One Minute Manager Builds High Performing Teams,* William Morrow and Company, Inc., New York, 1990.

Costanza, John R., *The Quantum Leap: In Speed to Market,* Third Edition, John Costanza Institute of Technology, Inc., Denver, Colorado, 1990.

Galsworth, Gwendolyn D., *The Visual Systems: Harnessing the Power of a Visual Workplace,* AMACOM, American Management Association, 1997.

Greif, Michel, *The Visual Factory: Building Participation Through Shared Information,* Productivity Press, Inc., Portland, Oregon, 1991.

Katzenbach, Jon R. and Smith, Douglas K., *The Wisdom of Teams: Creating the High-Performance Organization,* Harper Business – Division of Harper Collins Publishers, New York, New York, 1994.

Pande, Peter S., Neuman, Robert P. and Cavanagh, Roland R., *The Six Sigma Way,* McGraw-Hill Company, New York, New York, 2000.

Pitt, Hy, *SPC for the Rest of Us – A Personal Path to Statistical Process Control,* K. W. Tunnell Publishing Group, King of Prussia, PA, 1994.

Schonberger, Richard J., *World Class Manufacturing: The Next Decade, Building Power, Strength, and Value,* The Free Press, 1996.

Shigeo Shingo, *Zero Quality Control: Source Inspection and the Poka-yoke System,* Productivity Press, Stamford, CT and Cambridge, MA, 1986.

Womack, James P. and Jones, Daniel T., *Lean Thinking: Banish Waste and Create Wealth in Your Corporation,* Simon and Schuster, 1996.

I have included several appendices here that can be easily adapted to fit your own business improvement strategy. They pretty much follow the material presented in the book. Copy them, change them and turn them into your own presentations if you like. They are:
- Appendix A – Manufacturing – The factory
- Appendix B – Quality
- Appendix C – Self-Directed Teams
- Appendix D – Cost Savings Check List

RL BUCKLEY — Appendix A

Manufacturing
The Factory
R L Buckley

The Lean Path to
Continuous Improvement

RL BUCKLEY — The Way I See It

- Never let any subcontractor get close to your Customers
- Get your Low Cost Country (LCC) suppliers to use a local freight forwarder to hold inventory you can draw on -- Kanban
- Upper-level assembly, test, configuration in your own factory LCC or High Cost Country (HCC) – be the best here!!
- Distribution to customers from your own facilities –
- Be "World Class"
    - Highest quality - 99%+ first-pass yield – eliminate Out-of-Box Failures
    - Lowest possible cost - flow manufacturing
    - On-time delivery - within 5 day - first goal
    - Velocity (product throughput to 3 days)
    - Real self-directed work teams

RL BUCKLEY — Flow Manufacturing

Lean Flow Kanban pull system - no work orders
- Customer ⇐ finished goods ⇐ factory Kanban ⇐ vendor Kanban
- Linked cell manufacturing
- Inventory flexibility/reduction
- "In-house store", "Bread Man routine", "Wand to order"
- Point of use material delivery
- Certified vendors
- No WIP material -- cycle counting -- backflushing
- Manufacturing elements: labor, material, equipment
- Training – flexibility

RL BUCKLEY — 3 Ways To Build

Moving product and material through factory
1. Work order – push
   - Schedule in the future based on forecast
   - Kit material
   - Charge labor
   - Sometimes assign to equipment
2. Dispatching – push
   - Schedule in the future based on forecast
   - Pull material when ready to build
   - May or may not charge labor and assign equipment
3. Lean flow - Pull - Kanban signal – maximum flexibility
   - Build only when there is a demand
   - Pull material only when needed
   - Many other ways to charge labor

RL BUCKLEY   **Pull System**

- Customer places demand on finished goods
    - Finished goods demand fill causes signal
    - Signal causes factory demand
    - Factory demand fill causes signal
    - Signal causes vendor demand
    - Vendor demand fill causes signal
        - In-house store
        - Bread Man routine
        - Wand to order
    - Vendor signal fill creates PO – fills PO – creates Accounts Payable

RL BUCKLEY   **Linked Cell Manufacturing**

- Form each cell
    - U-shaped cells
    - Benches form the U
    - From left to right or right to left – be consistent
    - Define assembly flow – flow chart
    - Product size, number of parts, volume and demand variability will dictate cell size – 500 square feet is nice
    - Number of units per day
    - Design cell for flexibility
    - Link the cell by proximity to all the cells that supply this cell and also to the cell this cell supplies

RL BUCKLEY   Linked cell Kanbans

Linked cell signals
- Use one week – simple
- Use formula only when absolutely necessary
- Two-bin system is easiest
  - Bin travels as signal to make more
  - One weeks inventory between the bins
  - Use multiple bins to set priorities – FG Kanbans
    1. 5 of 5 bins part X back home – stock out!
    2. 4 of 5 bins part Y back home – make part 1 first
- Card Signal
  - Order point – 5 left then send card to make 10
  - Scan card sends message - intranet - internet – fax server

---

RL BUCKLEY   Inventory Flexibility/Reduction

- Create flexibility
  - Always have what I need when I need it!
  - I don't care when you make it – just have it when I need it!
- Make inventory your vendor's problem:
  - In-house stores
    - Consignment
  - Bread Man routine
  - Wand to order
- Increasing velocity pulls material through faster
- Make your LCC suppliers use freight forwarders to hold THEIR inventory

Use these techniques and watch your inventory disappear

RL BUCKLEY

Velocity

- Measured in days
- Starts when the first component is placed on board
- Ends when the unit is stocked
- Data must be collected automatically – Wanding
- When the unit is transacted to stock can look at history of longest lead assembly – usually the boards - use the birthing date
- The above requires a bar code assignment to the board fab when population is about to start – this is then the birthing date

RL BUCKLEY

In-house Store

- You provide designated floor space for material
- Vendor provides material
- Vendor provides Stock Keeper
- Also works for consignment material without Stock Keeper
- Vendor manages their inventory
- Scan into your inventory when delivered to your floor
- Vendor responsible for supplying inventory when you need it
- Vendor signal fill creates PO – fills PO – creates Accounts Payable
- Works well with electronic components, etc.
- Letter of intent with a partnering vendor

RL BUCKLEY   ## Bread Man Routine

- Used primarily for low value items
- Make your vendor responsible for filling all the blue bins or red bins or green bins, etc.
- Vendors visit daily - fill the bins that have reached fill level
- Vendor responsible for supplying inventory when you need it
- Vendor signal fill creates PO – fills PO – creates Accounts Payable
- Works well for nuts, bolts and screws, raw cable, resistors, etc.
- Letter of intent with a partnering vendor

RL BUCKLEY   ## Wand To Order

- Shop Floor operator uses bar code scanner to scan a Kanban bar code when a level is reached
- Message sent to PC or fax server
- Message sent to vendor
- Vendor delivers next day to Shop Floor (if certified part and certified vendor)
- Parts received with scanner Vendor responsible for supplying material when you need it
- Vendor signal fill creates PO – fills PO – creates Accounts Payable
- Works well with sheet-metal, packaging materials, circuit boards, cable assemblies, manuals, etc.
- Letter of intent with a partnering vendor

RL BUCKLEY — **Letter Of Intent**

- Letter of intent with a partnering vendor
  - Annual usage by part (within range) - access to your changing requirements
  - Pricing agreement
  - When pay – (50 to 60 days after taking possession)
  - Vendor must supply at the same or better price than you can buy anywhere – you must be reasonable
  - Can bundle commodities
  - Re-quote every year – ongoing
  - Provides for discontinuation responsibility

RL BUCKLEY — **Point Of Use**

- Deliver material to the work cell whenever possible
- Store inventory in the cell at the point of use
- Same parts used in more than one cell - highest usage gets the delivery – Production Associates access from other cells
- Keep Kanbans small enough
- Do not over stock
- May need warehouse for bulky items
- Warehouse linked to cell
- Never sacrifice efficiency in cell for storage
- Should be able to see all 4 walls

RL BUCKLEY — **Certified Vendors**

- Only certified vendors can deliver directly to the cell
- Certification program in line with your other quality programs
    - Historical quality record
    - ISO qualifications
    - On-site inspections
    - Questionnaire compliance
- After certifying vendor - must certify each part supplied – part's quality history and manufacturing location history
- Material not certified must be inspected according to current IQA criteria

RL BUCKLEY — **No WIP Material**

- Your factory becomes your stockroom
- All material is considered either:
    - Raw material
    - Finished goods
- Parts are scanned onto Shop Floor (stockroom) from:
    - In-house store
    - Bread Man – can be expensed
    - Wand to order delivery
- The backflushing process removes the material when finished goods is scanned to stock
- The material stocked in the cells is cycle counted daily to the cycle count plan – by cell Production Associates

RL BUCKLEY — ## Monitoring Labor Costs

Labor Absorption

- Use standard cost
- Know what you built
- Collect labor from time and attendance records
- Compare – unit standard X quantity built to hours worked
- Standard X quantity greater than hours worked = over absorbed
- Standard X quantity less that hours worked = under absorbed

---

RL BUCKLEY — ## Creating Flexibility

- Labor – material – equipment
- Equipment flexibility – given – not working 3 shifts 7 days a week – have equipment flexibility with OT
- Material flexibility – previously created material flexibility
- Labor flexibility – must be created with training

RL BUCKLEY

Labor Flexibility = Training

Today I built Mills. Yesterday I built boards. Tomorrow I will be winding film in the morning and testing fetal monitors in the afternoon. ===== THIS IS REAL!

- Reward for skills learned
- List employees and their skills – visible, well maintained
- Offer training on your time all the time
  - Plan it - schedule it - make training mandatory and optional
  - Training on entry
    - Flow manufacturing
    - Component Identification
    - As well as technical skills i.e. Soldering skills

RL BUCKLEY

Andon Lights

- 4" high by 30" long dot matrix displays products
- The product names either green, yellow, or red - depending on the production/shipping status
  - Yellow will indicate a pending problem
  - Green means go, no problems
  - Red will indicate unable to ship, all hands on deck
- Displayed in:
  - Purchasing   Q/A R/A
  - Cafeteria   Manufacturing
  - Order Management   Engineering
  - Management Offices Manufacturing Engineering
- Controlled by Shop Floor Supervisor

RL BUCKLEY — **Lean Manufacturing**

- **QA organization**
  - Eliminate QA inspectors
  - Don't build in lots, sort out rejects, use good ones
  - Statistical Process Control (SPC) put operator in charge of quality
  - Poka-yoke -- train all the people
- **Data collection -- bar code**
  - DHR, critical components
  - Backflushing
  - Kanban signals to vendor
  - Quality related tracking and identification (OBF, teams)
- **Warranty expense less than 1% of revenue**

RL BUCKLEY — **Lean Manufacturing**

To be "World Class"
Cannot rest on past accomplishments

- Inventory turns must be increased to 25
- On-time delivery increased to 100% level
- First-pass yield increased to 99%+
- Throughput time decreased to 3 to 4 days
- Warranty/scrap expense kept under 1%

RL BUCKLEY — Appendix B

Quality

Path to Continuous Improvement

R L Buckley

RL BUCKLEY — First-Pass Yield

Recommend a Team approach
- Measure after burn
- Plug the unit in and it works
- No tweaking
- Unit is ready to be configured
- 99% yield here reflects cumulative yield of all assemblies
- Keep it simple and Production Associates will manage it
- More than three failures in a cell in a day alerts Team members of a problem – should be automatic and electronic – to their desktop or pager/cell phone

Get this over 99% and Watch your OBFs disappear

RL BUCKLEY   **First-Pass Yield**

Quality related tracking and identification:
- Track each component that fails at final test
- Summarize and categorize all data
- Analyze and look for commonality
- Add Sub Assembly Groups to the Team
- Add vendors of problem parts to the Team
- Recommend Engineering changes
- Don't build assemblies in lots, sort out rejects, use good ones – build all assemblies in the final assembly cell
- SPC - put operator in charge of quality, if they are not already

Your Production Associates Will Be Key To Success

RL BUCKLEY   **First-Pass Yield**

Eliminate Workmanship Errors
- Poka-yoke the process -- train all the people
    - Make it formal
    - The course is inexpensive
    - You could teach it in house
        » About a 4 or 5 hour course
        » You can buy the course material
        . Simple and easy to understand examples
            . Your Production Associates will love it

Workmanship Errors Are The Easiest To Fix

RL BUCKLEY   ## Customer Quality Metrics

Customer's wants – the basics:
- Acceptable quality - on-time delivery - low cost
    - You control quality
    - You control delivery
    - You control cost
- You are concerned with all but try to measure what you control.
- DOA / OBF – Breakdown by:
    - » Design failures
    - » Random component failures
    - » No problem found
    - » Workmanship
    - Insist DOA / OBFs are returned
    - Insist on your Team reviewing DOA / OBF returns

RL BUCKLEY   ## Customer Quality Metrics

- Warranty expense:
    - Service breakdown by product
    - Difficult numbers to get – be persistent
    - Drive to less than 1%
- Install
    - Who gets this feedback?
    - What kind of feedback is available?
    - Website or questionnaire?
    - Select the data
    - This can be part of your closed loop feedback

Two Issues: Customer Satisfaction and Profits

RL BUCKLEY — Customer Quality/Satisfaction

- Delivery:
  - SPAN – this is the chosen metric for delivery
  - Ship Complete On Time (SCOT) to the Customer promise – do it!
    - Distinguishes your operation from the rest
    - Allows focus on the problem areas
      - Unreasonable promises
      - Unreleased product being sold
      - Product delayed from Low Cost Country (LCC)
      - Always ship complete
      - Need personal permission of Plant Manager to ship incomplete order - – - measure this
    - A short ship is an OBF – easy to fix

RL BUCKLEY — Six Sigma

Six Sigma Utilization

On The

Lean Path To Continuous Improvement

RL BUCKLEY — **Defining 6 Sigma**

What is Six Sigma?
- Measuring and eliminating the variations in any process.
- Sigma = standard deviation
    - 2 sigma   308,537   DPMO
    - 3 sigma   66,807   DPMO
    - 4 sigma   6210   DPMO
    - 5 sigma   233   DPMO
    - 6 sigma   3.4   DPMO

Improve your process 3 sigma to 6 sigma - 20,000 times improvement!

Which airplane do you want to fly on?

RL BUCKLEY — **6 Sigma Methodology?**

Why do we care about 6 Sigma methodology?

- If you can't measure or you don't measure, you will never know and understand your process
- If you don't know and understand your processes, you will never control or improve your processes
- You will forever be relying on chance and dumb luck

RL BUCKLEY — Serving Your Customers

Deliver:

Higher quality products

At a lower cost

On-time – when your Customer wants them

Be The Best – Leap Frog Your Competition

RL BUCKLEY — Areas Of 6 Sigma Application

- Manufacturing
- Engineering – product design
- Back office
    - Order Management
    - Finance
    - Collections and Payables
    - e-business
    - RA/QA
- Marketing & Sales
- Service

Apply To All Business Functions – Identify Deviations From The Ideal

RL BUCKLEY — What Is In It For Your People?

Not just fun – and it is fun!!

- An investment in your employees
- Personal growth
- Everybody wants to be the best and work for the best
- Attract the best
- A skill that is in high demand
- Eliminate the politics in project decisions

RL BUCKLEY — Some Of The 6 Sigma Tools

Examples of tools used:

- ✓ Benchmarking
- ✓ Brainstorming
- ✓ Control charts
- ✓ Capability analysis
- ✓ Histogram – frequency distribution
- ✓ Pareto – sort vital few from trivial many
- ✓ QFD Quality function deployment – VOC in design
- ✓ FMEA – failure mode and effects analysis
- ✓ Gage R&R – Gage repeatability and reproductibility
- ✓ Process Mapping
- ✓ DOE – Design of experiments
- ✓ C & E – Cause and Effect

RL BUCKLEY

"The problems that exist in the world of today...

...Cannot be solved by the level of thinking that created them."
Albert Einstein

RL BUCKLEY   **Appendix C**

Self-Directed Teams

Path to Continuous Improvement

R L Buckley

RL BUCKLEY   **Self-Directed Teams**

- Establish a challenge -- Should be established by the person forming the Team. The following are examples for self-directed (cross-functional) Teams:
    - 1. Reduce inventory by $10,000,000 by the end of the year
    - 2. Improve on-time delivery hit rate to the 99%+ level over the next year
    - 3. Eliminate the use of Shop Floor work orders by December
    - 4. Automate the Data Collection systems on the Manufacturing Floor - up and running by January 1
- Each Team is composed of: a Team Leader - appointed; a Facilitator - appointed; a Secretary to keep minutes - elected; and the Team members
- Team size usually should be more than 5 less than 12

RL BUCKLEY — **Self-Directed Teams**

- Teams should meet at least once a week
- When Teams accomplish their goals, the Team will be disbanded
- Team must create an infrastructure that will survive the Team effort so that the accomplishments of the Team will continue to bear fruit
- Team sets goals and assigns tasks to meet the challenge
- Each Team is empowered to draw on the talents and expertise in the Company (this includes the entire organization) on a part-time basis. For example: If help is required from the Sourcing Group to get vendor quotes, a buyer will be assigned to the Team until the quoting is complete

---

RL BUCKLEY — **Self-Directed Teams**

- Team meeting attendance and showing up on time is both important and mandatory in order to maintain Team member status

- Teams are expected to give progress reports to a senior manager (the more senior the better) in the form of a Team presentation

- Governance ground rules should be established up front – at the first or second meeting - by the Team, as the Team deems necessary. The ground rules could cover majority rule, attendance, etc.

RL BUCKLEY — Appendix D

Cost Savings Check List

Path to Continuous Improvement
R L Buckley

RL BUCKLEY — Cost Savings Check List 1

- Labor hours
  - Overtime reduction
  - Temps, contractors
  - Process improvement
  - Shift elimination
- Outsource – vendor does it at a lower cost
- Review all equipment leases
  - Copiers
  - Shipping dock
  - Trucks & cars
  - Storage trailers

RL BUCKLEY — **Cost Savings Check List 2**

- Services
  - Carpets
  - Equipment servicing
    - Fork trucks
    - Bailers
- Off-site storage
  - Building leases
- Scrap
- Quote boards and/or assemblies outside
- Shop supplies
  - ESD Shop Coats
  - Small tools – add to in-house stores

RL BUCKLEY — **Cost Savings Check List 3**

- Depreciation
  - Unneeded assets that can be transferred or sold
  - Non-existent assets
- Freight
  - Look for vendors with several freight charges on the same day. Charging freight for two deliveries when both items came in the same box.
  - When we pay the freight – only when we agreed
  - When ship – ship lowest cost – etc.
- Calibration
  - Outside vs. inside
  - Remove unused items from service
- Utilities
  - Phones – cell phones
  - Electric
  - Water
  - Gas

RL BUCKLEY   **Cost Savings Check List 4**

- Housekeeping
- Obsolescence
- Product packaging
- Travel & Entertainment
- Discretionary meetings
- Supplies
- Shop Floor space you pay for and maybe don't use
- Cafeteria contributions – is it allocated?
- Other allocated expenses you do not control
- Purchase costs
    - CDs - inside or outside
    - Manuals - inside or outside